THE LIVING MEMORIAL

Committee Members

Morry Weiss, *Chairman*
Harry M. Brown, *President*

Rabbi Eli Dessler
Rabbi Yitzchak Kasnett, M.S.
Rabbi A. Leib Scheinbaum
Ivan Soclof
Rabbi Sholom Strajcher
Rabbi Sholom Ziskind
Arlene Jaffe, MSSA, LISW
Leatrice B. Rabinsky, Ph.D.

Unit I:
The World That Was

Section I:
Lithuania

A Study of the Life and Torah Consciousness of Jews
in the Towns and Villages of Lithuania
and Northeastern Poland

by Rabbi Yitzchak Kasnett

THE LIVING MEMORIAL
A Curriculum developed by the Hebrew Academy Of Cleveland

The Living Memorial Project
is dedicated in memory of

Harry and Gizi Weiss

צבי בן יואל ע"ה
גיטל בת ישראל ע"ה

by their loving children
Morry & Judy Weiss
Erwin & Myra Weiss

Their faith in the Almighty sustained them through the fires of the Holocaust. They came to America and rebuilt a life committed to their heritage. They valued a Jewish education and this legacy lives on. Their devotion to each other and to their family will always serve as an inspiration to their children and grandchildren, in whose hearts their memory will live on forever.

The Living Memorial
Unit I: The World That Was
Section I: Lithuania
First Printing...October 1996
Second Printing...October 1997

© Copyright 1996, by The Living Memorial, in conjunction with the Hebrew Academy of Cleveland
All rights reserved. No part of this book may be reproduced in any form or with any technology, without
the express written authorization from the publisher.
ISBN: 0-9635120-8-0

Published by:
The Living Memorial
c/o Hebrew Academy of Cleveland
1860 South Taylor Road
Cleveland Heights, Ohio 44118
216-321-5838 ext. 165
Fax: 216-321-0588

Distributed by:
Mesorah Publications, Ltd.
4401 Second Avenue
Brooklyn, New York 11232
718-921-9000
800-MESORAH
Fax: 718-680-1875

Designed and produced by:
Yitzchok Saftlas/Bottom Line Design
718-332-8134

Printed in the United States of America

Photo Credits:
The Living Memorial is grateful to the following individuals and organizations for making their photo collections available for this project: Shlomie Abraham; Menachem Adelman; Agudath Israel Archives/ Rabbi Moshe Kolodny; Rabbi Nochum Zev Dessler; Rebbetzin Zlota Ginsburg; Rabbi Eliezer Ginsburg; Rabbi Yitzchok Kasnett; Dr. Leatrice Rabinsky; Eliyohu Saftlas; Yitzchok Saftlas; Zev Saftlas; Dovid Turkel.

The publisher has made every effort to determine and locate the owners of the additional photos used in this publication. Please notify The Living Memorial in case of accidental omission.

In Appreciation

This ambitious project required the generous support of many people to make it a reality. We are grateful to all those who enabled us to do so. We especially recognize and pay tribute to **Morry and Judy Weiss**, who launched this project with love, awe and conviction. Their mission to hold dear the memory of the victims of the Holocaust, to create an everlasting memorial, so that future generations will reflect with pride upon their ancestors, inspired them as they inspired us. They follow in the noble tradition of the Patriarch of their family, **Mr. Irving Stone**, who together with his wife, **Helen**, have become legends in the field of Torah education and philanthropy. No project is too great, no endeavor too small, if it will promote and enhance the study of Torah and if it will effect a stronger and more vibrant *Am Yisrael*, they are at the forefront. Lovingly called *"Mr. Hebrew Academy,"* Irving Stone has always been there from the very beginning, as a caring and loving father nurturing his child to maturity, sharing in the joy of its success.

We are deeply indebted to **Mr. Leonard Stern** and the **Stern Family Foundation** for graciously investing our vision, to develop and publish this curriculum. Mr. Stern came forward during the project's inception providing support and encouragement. His confidence in our work has meant a great deal to us. In addition, we are especially grateful to **Richard & Amelia Bernstein; Max Fisher; George Klein; and Sam & Arie Halpern** for sponsoring The Living Memorial's educational programs. Their friendship and support has been vital to our success.

To all those who have given assistance and offered counsel; to the thousands of students, teachers and principals throughout the country who have implemented our programs; to the parents and grandparents who encouraged us, we say — Thank You. May the Almighty guide and inspire us that this volume be the forerunner of a curriculum that will illuminate and pay tribute to an era that was lost but never forgotten.

 **PREFACE**

זכור את אשר עשה עמלק

"Remember what Amalek did to you!"
(Devarim 25:17)

ow do we go about remembering what Amalek did to us if we do not really understand the magnitude of the destruction he wrought? Where does one place his focus of remembrance? If we are to remember, it must serve a purpose. While remembrance has its obligations, it also has its priorities and parameters.

The goal of The Living Memorial has been to focus our remembrance upon an aspect of the Holocaust, which is regretfully being forgotten. When the Nazi beast decimated European Jewry, he destroyed more than human lives. Together with the six million souls who perished in the most cruel manner, a culture was destroyed that was majestic and noble, yet warm and unpretentious. European Jewry took on many forms which reflected several diverse approaches to the Torah way of life. There were the pure hearts and warm spirits of Chassidic Jewry; the dignity and refinement that characterizes German Jewry; the profound faith and courage of Hungarian Jewry; the purity, modesty and incisive Torah minds that personifies Lithuanian Jewry; the sincerity and joy of life of Russian Jewry; the charm and graciousness of Galician Jewry; the commitment to age-old tradition that was demonstrated by the Balkan Jews; and the exciting multi-dimensional world of Polish Jewry.

These "worlds" were all part of the "universe" of European Jewry. Each represented a microcosm of pure Jewish values which combined to create a heritage and legacy unparalleled in Jewish history. It is our mandate to remember and reflect upon this unique world, to critically examine its distinctiveness, so that we can begin to understand the destruction of European Jewry.

It is only after extensive research into the "world that was" that we can more fully grasp the magnitude of the Holocaust, how deeply we suffered then and the terrible loss which we still feel today. Remembering the way of life of our ancestors, their spiritual heroism against all odds, serves as a powerful example to us. It is our moral obligation, and spiritual legacy to preserve and transmit these memories, so that the values and way of life of the martyrs will endure.

Many of our youth are well acquainted with the more notable Torah luminaries of the past generation. Their personalities, ideals, aspirations and accomplishments serve as an example for us to aspire to emulate. It is regarding the *"poshute Yid"* — the ordinary Jew, the *"bubehs and zaidehs"* of yesterday, that little has yet been acknowledged.

The noble life style and spiritual majesty of the ordinary Jew of past generations has not been recorded. Beneath their torn and tattered clothing existed great and

It is only after extensive research into the "world that was" that we can more fully grasp the magnitude of the Holocaust, how deeply we suffered then and the terrible loss which we still feel today.

It is our moral obligation, and spiritual legacy to preserve and transmit these memories, so that the values and way of life of the martyrs will endure.

holy souls filled with Torah study and *mitzvah* performance. Their moral characteristics would serve as an example of holiness, while their devotion to acts of loving-kindness knew no bounds. The saga of our parents and grandparents of European descent serve as a wellspring of Jewish inspiration to future generations.

It is our hope that by studying the life and times of the past generation, our children/students, many of whom unfortunately did not have the opportunity to meet and develop a relationship with grandparents, will realize their spiritual roots. This realization will instill a sense of pride, heighten awareness and inspire them to continue to build upon the foundation which was tempered by their ancestors. Come join with us as we delve into this "world that was" so that we may learn to appreciate our Heritage.

The focus of this work is based upon the oral and written perspectives of some of the most notable and prolific thinkers and writers of the past and present.

The focus of this work is based upon the oral and written perspectives of some of the most notable and prolific thinkers and writers of the past and present. Presented herein will be a Torah-oriented appreciation of the "world that was". It will relate the way of life in the more famous communities in the European spectrum of Jewish life.

Acknowledgments

For a project of this magnitude to be successful it demands inspiration, conviction and commitment.

The inspiration came from **Morry Weiss**, whose idea and dream it was to provide a Holocaust-oriented curriculum for the Yeshiva Day School student so that the "world that was"—the world into which he was born—would never be forgotten. He gave up much of his personal time and attention, despite his heavy schedule. He has been both parent and friend to this project throughout its tenure.

The conviction came from **Harry M. Brown**, president of the The Living Memorial. His belief in the project's success, and his sense of obligation to the Holocaust victims spurred us on, while it helped us overcome the challenges in our path.

Commitment is what kept us going. **Rabbi Yitzchak Kasnett** started out as curriculum writer and became so intensely involved in every aspect of the project that he has redefined the word commitment.

Rabbi Nochum Zev Dessler, Shlita, Dean, Hebrew Academy of Cleveland,, was our spiritual mentor. A scion of the Lithuanian Mussar dynasty, he "lives" the "world that was".

Arlene Jaffe, our Director of Development, has toiled throughout the entire project, keeping us on schedule, seeing to it that we never lost sight of where we were going and never gave up hope.

Yitzchok Saftlas designed a volume of pure visual delight. Inspired by the emotions and persona of that era, his efforts have created a symmetry between word and design.

The Hebrew Academy of Cleveland spearheaded this project and has set the standard for Torah-oriented curricula. We are grateful to **Rabbi Sholom Strajcher**, its Educational Director, during whose tenure this project saw fruition. His expertise in Jewish education has been of great assistance to us. **Ivan Soclof**, President of the Hebrew Academy, has been a guiding force in the realization of this curriculum. His propensity for detail kept our goal in perspective.

We are honored that **Dr. Leatrice B. Rabinsky**, noted Holocaust historian and author, who has devoted her life to teaching the Holocaust to thousands of students, has joined us to co-author parts of the curriculum.

Last, but not least, we are grateful to Torah Umesorah, the National Society for Hebrew Day Schools, and its Director, **Rabbi Joshua Fishman**, for their advice, support and encouragement throughout this endeavor.

We pray to *Hashem* that our work will truly serve as a *"Living Memorial"* to the victims of the Holocaust.

> **Rabbi A. Leib Scheinbaum**
> *National Director, The Living Memorial*
> *Elul, 5756 / September 1996*

We pray to Hashem that our work will truly serve as a "Living Memorial" to the victims of the Holocaust.

⇒ AUTHOR'S PREFACE

he World That Was... the world of the Orthodox Jew of Eastern Europe before World War II has, in so many ways, taught me that each life, each Jewish soul, is a complete world, an עולם השלם. Each of us is always so busy with our own tasks and responsibilities that not only do we not take the time to appreciate the depth, richness and meaning of another's life, but even regarding our own lives we hardly show appreciation for the great gift Hashem has bestowed upon us. Each interview left me changed as an individual, and now that the project is drawing to its conclusion I have the time to reflect upon those individuals, those wonderful Jews whose lives are made of a fabric and color that we rarely see today.

In truth, this project is a "living memorial," for it will be the rare individual who will read these pages, share these lives, and not be changed by doing so...

It is essential for the student to approach the reading of these interviews from the unique perspective of life presented by each of our interviewees. Therefore, the student should actively project him or herself into their thoughts and emotions, their mind's eye view of life. For this you will be rewarded with the ability to transcend the decades of time and the barriers of social change that have ensued to capture and experience, at least in some small measure, their clear, unobstructed view of a Jew's purpose in life, a life of striving for spiritual purity and closeness to Torah.

This project is sponsored by The Living Memorial and the Hebrew Academy of Cleveland. In truth, this project is a "living memorial," for it will be the rare individual who will read these pages, share these lives, and not be changed by doing so—reflecting upon the values and beliefs lived and expressed by our interviewees. In my own family we now have a new perspective with which to measure our actions and desires. Whenever one of us wants to do something, or buy something, we ask, "And what would they say in Kelm about this?" What would those pure, striving souls say about much of our behavior and aspirations?

This has been a wonderful experience for me personally, and, by extension, for my family as well. I would like to thank my wife, Shulamis, for her insightful comments and suggestions from the beginning of the project to its conlusion. Her appreciation of the importance of this curriculum, and her personal support and understanding during its development over the past 2½ years have been invaluable.

There are many people who make a project of this magnitude come to fruition. I list them here and thank all of them for their involvement and support:

Rabbi N. Z. Dessler, *Dean and Founder, The Hebrew Academy of Cleveland*

Morry Weiss, *Chairman and Founder of The Living Memorial*

Harry M. Brown, *President of The Living Memorial*

Rabbi A. Leib Scheinbaum, *National Director of The Living Memorial*

Arlene Jaffe, *Director of Development for The Living Memorial*

Dr. Leatrice Rabinsky, *Co-author*

Yitzchok Saftlas, *graphic design & layout / Bottom Line Design*

Rabbi Moshe Kolodny, *Archivist / Agudath Israel of America*

Selma Hellman, *Editor*

Ethel Gottlieb, *Editor*

Blima Levine, *Typist*

Together we have tried, with G-d's blessing, to produce a curriculum that does, in more than small measure, capture the essence of a time in our history that was literally wiped off the face of the earth. Our interviewees are our bridges to a past that is slowly coming to its end. We thank them for bequeathing to us their living memorial in their lifetimes, and in the merit of their great deeds may they be granted long life, and serve as bridges to the future redemption as well.

Rabbi Yitzchak Kasnett
Elul 5756 / September 1996

Together we have tried, with G-d's blessing, to produce a curriculum that does, in more than small measure, capture the essence of a time in our history that was literally wiped off the face of the earth.

〰 TABLE OF CONTENTS

TORAH UMESORAH
תורה ומסורה

The National Society
for Hebrew Day Schools

COMMITTING GENERATIONS TO TORAH

19 Elul 5756
September 3, 1996

Rabbi N.W. Dessler, Dean
Hebrew Academy of Cleveland
1860 South Taylor Road
Cleveland Heights, Ohio 44118

Dear Rabbi Dessler,

I had the great privilege to read the appreciation of Yahadus Lita which is being published by the Hebrew Academy of Cleveland.

On a personal level I must tell you that you are the mentor and teacher who introduced me to the world of Lithuanian Jewry in a meaningful way. I was of course privileged to listen to Shmuessen from some of the Gedolei Baalei Hamussar of our time. From them I heard profound insights and great teachings. From you Reb Velvel אלופי ומיודעי through the privilege of a long association in the world of chinuch, I heard of the הליכות יום יום of the Baalei Mussar, their sensibilities, sensitivities, depth of thinking, profound consideration even for the least of G-d's creatures and above all their עקשנות, in the face of a decadent world, to strive for excellence and elevated spirituality.

This important work is a wonderful depiction of the greatness and the "eidelkeit" of Lithuanian Jewry. This volume is a great resource for our children for generations to come.

On behalf of generations of talmidim of Torah Umesorah schools, I thank you.

Sincerely,

Rabbi Joshua Fishman
Executive Vice President

160 BROADWAY, 4th Fl.
NEW YORK, NY 10038
TEL: (212) 227-1000
FAX: (212) 406-6934
E-mail: umesorah @ aol.com

≈ TORAH:

Excerpts from an interview with the Rosh HaYeshiva of Telz
Rabbi Mordecai Gifter, Shlita

YK: Why did the Rosh HaYeshiva decide to go to Telz to learn?

Rabbi Gifter: My uncle felt that it would be beneficial for me to learn there.

YK: How did the Rosh HaYeshiva's parents respond to such a suggestion, that Rabbi Gifter should leave Baltimore at 16 and go to Lithuania?

Rabbi Gifter: My father wanted me to go, but my mother was somewhat hesitant. I traveled by ship to France, and then went overland by train to Lithuania.

YK: What main impression does the Rosh HaYeshiva have of his first experience in Telz?

Rabbi Gifter: I was a youngster. I walked into the Beis Hamedrash and I saw Torah! There were 500 boys sitting and learning and no one was wasting any time! In Lithuania you saw Torah—that Torah was all of one's life.

"I walked into the Beis Hamedrash and I saw Torah! There were 500 boys sitting and learning and no one was wasting any time!"

In his first few minutes in Telz, the Rosh HaYeshiva was able to perceive that the great majority of Orthodox Jews in the towns and villages of Lithuania and Poland valued Torah study above all else. We now proceed to study and reflect upon the rest of the material of this chapter, a study that will hopefully lead the student to a greater appreciation and understanding of the life of Torah that so impressed Rabbi Gifter as a young American teenager of 16 in 1933. Only through such effort can we attempt to recapture, in some measure, the Torah consciousness of the Jewish world that existed so recently in our history, but is no more.

Yitzchok Saftlas

Rabbi Mordecai Gifter, Shlita, Rosh HaYeshiva of Telz

...the great majority of Orthodox Jews in the towns and villages of Lithuania and Poland valued Torah study above all else.

≋ INTRODUCTION:

Perspectives of spiritual greatness—
An appreciation of the spiritual world of Eastern Europe

he following interviews were held with the Telzer Rosh HaYeshiva, Rabbi Mordecai Gifter, *Shlita,* and his Rebbetzin; Rabbi Avigdor Miller, *Shlita;* Rabbi Nochum Zev Dessler, *Shlita;* and Rebbetzin Zlota Ginsburg. The major portion of this section is comprised of the interview with Rebbetzin Ginsburg, who gave generously of her time to provide a thorough and detailed narrative of daily life in the towns and villages of Lithuania and Poland from the turn of the century until World War II. The Telzer Rosh HaYeshiva, Rabbi Miller and Rabbi Dessler graciously gave of their time to provide the student with singular perspectives of the spiritual dimensions of Torah life and study in the yeshivos of Lithuania. All of our interviewees contributed to this project because of their strong conviction that such information is critical to the proper education of today's yeshiva student.

These interviews allow us to experience the phenomena of pre-World War II life in the smaller towns of Lithuania and Poland while being exposed to many of the Torah luminaries of that era.

The student has been provided with an accurate first-hand account of this important period in Jewish history by those who lived in Europe. These interviews will provide future generations with a sensitive, wise, and, at times, even humorous narrative that captures both the material

deprivation and spiritual greatness of the Jews of that era. Rabbi Yosef Leib Bloch, the Telzer Rov and Rosh HaYeshiva (see the History of Telz), taught that an increase in materialism inhibits intellectual growth, eventually diminishing one's greatness in Torah and faith. Thus, the poverty so prevalent in Eastern Europe provided the appropriate spiritual environment for greatness in Torah, particularly when one considers the number of outstanding *gaonim,* depth of Torah learning, and the great yearning for spiritual perfection and closeness to G-d that existed as the *raison d'etre* for both student and common folk alike.

This is the priceless legacy bequeathed to us from those previous generations. We, today, must try to emulate their Torah consciousness, their striving for holiness, their love for G-d and each fellow Jew. We can never recreate the past, but we can try to learn how past generations practiced their values. Then we can try to transfer these values to the world in which we live.

Many people in the small towns and villages felt that life without Torah was not really living; believing, not that in life there was Torah, but, conversely, that Torah was life, and without Torah what one lived could not really be called a life. The following story illustrates this philosophy.[1]

Shimon, a slightly built Chassidic boy, was 11-years-old when he entered the Lodz (Litzmanstadt) Ghetto with his

These interviews will provide future generations with a sensitive, wise, and, at times, even humorous narrative that captures both the material deprivation and spiritual greatness of the Jews of that era.

---

1. Adapted from an article in the **"Yated Ne'eman,"** 1/20/95; Vol 7, No. 3.

family over 50 years ago. The disruption of normal life and the abysmal conditions surrounding him didn't succeed in altering Shimon's spirit. He acted on a regular basis as an agent, who brought food from a compassionate gentile to an elderly Jew in the ghetto.

One day Shimon was caught and beaten mercilessly by three Gestapo men who wanted him to reveal the name of the gentile who "illegally" supplied the life-sustaining food for the old Jew. Other men who were apprehended and beaten for a variety of meaningless reasons received 100 lashes, but little Shimon, who remained standing and silent, was given 125 lashes.

The three Gestapo men were utterly bewildered by the silent courage of this child who wouldn't reveal the name of the food supplier. They aimed their rifles towards Shimon in a desperate attempt to force him to talk. It would have been so easy for Shimon to reveal the name of the food supplier. Even if Shimon did reveal the name, the Gestapo probably would not find their prey. Who would blame this tortured child for revealing the name?

Little Shimon remained impervious to the ominous clicks that meant the rifles would soon be fired. He closed his eyes, recited "Shema Yisrael," and the "Viduy," the last confessional prayers. These same prayers were uttered by Jewish martyrs who perished in the burning pyres of the Spanish Inquisition. The same prayers offered throughout history by Jews who were willing to sacrifice their lives in order to preserve the sanctity of their souls.

But Shimon did not die. He remained standing with his eyes closed, immersed in his final prayers long after the Gestapo put down their guns and withdrew. It was only when someone came and told him to go home that Shimon realized his life was spared. Shimon suffered for weeks afterwards from the brutal beating that he received, and there was not a spot on his body that was not bruised and swollen, but his soul remained unscathed.

Shimon never thought he did anything remarkable, and it was only after ten years of marriage that he mentioned this incident to his wife. Shimon said that he refused to divulge the name of the food supplier because he could not repay the gentile's kindness with betrayal. That would have been contrary to the teachings of the Torah.

How many children of 11-years-old would be able to grasp the essence of Torah as did Shimon 50 years ago? Did Shimon's strength come from the Torah consciousness instilled in him in a Jewish town where Torah was the sole justification for life?

> *Shimon never thought he did anything remarkable...he could not repay the gentile's kindness with betrayal. That would have been contrary to the teachings of the Torah.*

This is the priceless legacy bequeathed to us from those previous generations...

In the introduction of his book, **Atlas of the Holocaust,**[2] Martin Gilbert writes the following commentary about one of the 316 maps he drew chronicling the destruction of European Jewry:

"This map shows the birthplaces, places of work, and places of execution of 17 Jews who were murdered during the war years. The text which follows on this page tells, briefly, something of their personal stories. If a similarly short reference were made to each Jew murdered between 1939 and 1945, 353,000 such maps would be needed. *To draw these maps at the author's and cartographer's fastest rate of a map a day, would take more than 967 years.*"

Map 316, on page 244, lists an estimated number of Jews killed during World War II in Europe. A ***partial*** reading from map 316 appears in the chart to the right:

Poland	3,000,000
Soviet Union	1,000,000
Hungary	305,000
Czechoslovakia	277,000
Germany	160,000
Lithuania	135,000
Holland	106,000
France	83,000
Latvia	80,000
Austria	65,000
Greece	65,000
Yugoslavia	60,000
Italy	8,000
Rhodes	1,700
Danzig	1,000
Albania	200
Kos	120
Denmark	77
Finland	11

In Section I, we begin our study of pre-war life in the Lithuanian Jewish communities, focusing on the great Torah centers and personalities of the latter 19th century to the time of their destruction by the Nazis.

---

2. Gilbert, Martin, **Atlas of the Holocaust,** William Morrow, New York, 1988, pages 10 and 244

EUROPE BEFORE WORLD WAR II

✑ TEACHER'S GUIDE/ INTRODUCTORY STUDENT EXERCISES

...for enhancing the understanding of the Historical Portraits of Mir, Telz and Vilna

LESSON 1:

- ❏ Teacher directed lesson
- ❏ Consider concepts of *size* and *importance* from a spiritual perspective

Materials

- ❏ 2 copies of Work Sheet #1 per student

MIR:

A. Exercise One

1. Draw a circle approximately 1/8th of an inch in diameter in the middle of the box on Work Sheet #1. Consider the relative size and importance of the circle in relation to the rest of the area of the paper. Does the circle assume a position of dominance on the paper?

2. Repeat this exercise using the second copy of Work Sheet #1, only draw the circle in the lower left hand corner of the box.

3. Place the two Work Sheets next to each other and compare the two papers. On which Work Sheet does the circle assume the greatest importance? Why?

Most students will respond that it is the *position* and not the *size* of the circle on the first Work Sheet that makes it important, because if it were a bigger circle it would be prominent even in the corner of the Work Sheet.

B. Exercise Two

1. As Jews, what principle do we often find in life that is expressed through this exercise? You may discuss this question together with your classmates. After you have composed your answer, write it on a sheet of paper. (From here we will refer to this principle as the *Yeshiva Principle* since we have derived it from our study of the Lithuanian yeshivos.)

2. Have several students read their statements of principle to the class. Then write a statement that expresses the majority sentiment of the class. Each individual may still retain his/her unedited statement of principle.

Sample answers:

1. Often it is not the size or strength of something that bestows upon it its sense of importance, it is the position it holds in the life of a person or in the history of a nation. Not always are our largest or most expensive possessions the ones most important to us.

2. Importance is not judged by external characteristics such as size, beauty, strength or wealth, etc., but by the vital role that the object (person, place or thing) plays in the quality of life and well-being of the person or people it affects.

Homework Assignment:

Geography, demographics and map skills:

A. In which countries were the following yeshivos located before WWII?
    1. Kelm
    2. Kletzk
    3. Mir
    4. Slobodka
    5. Telz

B. Were these yeshivos in cities or towns?

C. How large are the counties in which these yeshivos were located? Answer in square miles.

D. What is the capital city of each country?

E. What are the three largest cities in each country?

F. What language or languages are spoken in each country?

G. What is the major religion in each country?

H. List the major geographical features of each country.

I. If it is 12:00 noon in your city, what time is it in the capital city in one of these countries?

J. How many miles is it from your location to the capital city in one of these countries?

Student Exercises

WORK SHEET #1

Student: _____ **Date:** _____

Class: _____ **Instructor:** _____

Follow your instructor's directions for using the box below. Ask for additional copies if needed.

LESSON 2:

- ❑ Teacher directed lesson
- ❑ Review *Yeshiva Principle* and homework from Lesson 1
- ❑ Focus on map skills

Materials:

- ❑ One completed map of Poland (Work Sheet #2) and Lithuania (Work Sheet #4)
- ❑ Four blank maps of each country per student (Work Sheet #3, Poland; and #5, Lithuania)

A. Exercise One

1. Review *Yeshiva Principle* and homework from Lesson 1

B. Exercise Two

Extend discussion of *Yeshiva Principle* in Lesson 1 by leading the students to appreciate that while these towns were geographically small and insignificant in size, no match for the cultural and social centers of European life at that time, such as Paris, Vienna, Berlin, Milan, Rome, Prague or Budapest, nonetheless, they stand out as major cities of the world on the Heavenly Map of earth. The same holds true for Radin, Ponevezh, Satmar, Nitra, etc. As Jews we measure greatness by a different standard, one which is almost completely foreign to the rest of the world. Though great museums, palaces, hotels, plazas and opera houses may determine the importance of a city by world standards, Jews measure the greatness of a city or town by the spiritual giants who, together with their *talmidim* and townspeople, build structures of spiritual purity that is the lifeblood of existence for the Jewish people and the whole of creation.

C. Exercise Three

1. Distribute copies of the completed maps of Poland and Lithuania (Work Sheets #2 and #4) to the students, pointing out the major Torah centers. [Optional for teacher: distribute more detailed maps, including population densities and topographic features, etc.]

2. Distribute four blank maps (Work Sheets #3 and #5) to the students. Ask the class to replicate the features from the finished maps to the blank maps for each country. Inform the class that they will be responsible for the completion of such an activity in the future without benefit of the completed maps.

Homework Assignment:

1. Review the answers to the map questions.

2. If not finished in class, complete the blank maps of Poland and Lithuania by replicating the features presented on the completed maps.

3. Complete each of the maps again, this time only filling in the major cities of each country as well as the yeshiva cities and towns.

WORK SHEET #2

Student: _____ Date: _____

Class: _____ Instructor: _____

POLAND: CITIES & TOWNS

Baltic Sea

LITHUANIA

GERMANY

GERMANY
(EAST PRUSSIA)

• Vilna

• Radin

• Volozhin

Grodna •

Mir •

Baranovitch •

• Lomza

Slonim •

Kletzk

• Kamenitz

Pinsk

Brisk •

Warsaw •   • Minsk

Ger •

P O L A N D

Lodz •

• Novardok

Karlin

• Lublin

Chelm

Rowne

• Kielce

Belz •   River Bug

Dubno •

Vistula River

Crakow

• Tarnow

Lvov (Lemberg)

Oswiecim
(Auschwitz)   • Bobov

Tarnopol •

Czortkow •

C Z E C H O S L O V A K I A

Student Exercises

WORK SHEET #3

Student: _____ Date: _____

Class: _____ Instructor: _____

Identify the unlabeled cities and towns.

POLAND: CITIES & TOWNS

Baltic Sea

LITHUANIA

GERMANY

GERMANY
(EAST PRUSSIA)

Grodna ●

Slonim ●

P O L A N D

● Kielce

Vistula River

River Bug

Rowne

● Tarnow

Tarnopol ●

Czortkow ●

C Z E C H O S L O V A K I A

WORK SHEET #4

Student: _____ Date: _____

Class: _____ Instructor: _____

LITHUANIAN CITIES & TOWNS

WORK SHEET #5

Student: _____   Date: _____

Class: _____   Instructor: _____

Identify the major Torah centers indicated on this map.

LITHUANIAN CITIES & TOWNS

Baltic Sea

Riga •

LATVIA

• Dvinsk

L I T H U A N I A

• Köenigsberg

GERMANY
(EAST PRUSSIA)

POLAND

LESSON 3:

❏ Review answers to geography questions and student maps of Poland and Lithuania

Materials:

❏ Student copies of historical sketches to be handed out as each town is studied.

Exercise One

❏ Begin study of the histories of Mir, Telz and Vilna.

Mir, located in eastern Poland between the two World Wars, was geographically small in size... yet it remains a location of huge spiritual prominence on the Jewish map of the world.

MIR

ir, located in eastern Poland between the two World Wars, was geographically small in size, with a 1921 Jewish population of 2,074 people, yet it remains a location of huge spiritual prominence on the Jewish map of the world. Mir was a town in Grodno Oblast (a territorial administrative district) in the Byelorussian province of the Soviet Socialist Republic. Byelarussia is the western part of European Russia (bordering on Eastern Poland), an area of 89,300 square miles, with a population of approximately 5,568,000, whose capital is the city of Minsk.[3]

From 1569 until the early 1800s the town of Mir and the surrounding lands belonged to the Radziwill princes. The Jews of Mir became an important part of the local trade, and were major sources of commerce at the two annual trade fairs held in Mir. Jewish merchants from every part of Lithuania and Poland were attracted to the fairs in Mir, where they carried on an extensive trade in furs, horses, oxen, spices, grain, textiles, tobacco (from 1672) and wine. In the records of the Lithuania Council, Mir is mentioned for the first time in 1662. Records show that from 1673 Lithuanian Jews paid taxes to state institutions and debts to other creditors that were occasionally collected at the Mir fairs.

During the early decades of the 18th century, the Jewish population of Mir increased considerably. The local Jewish contribution to the poll tax rose from 45 zlotys in 1673 to 1,160 zlotys in 1700, and 1,350 zlotys in 1720. During this period the merchants of Mir maintained fruitful commercial relations with Leipzig, Koenigsberg, Memel and Libau. In 1697, 1702 and 1751, the community leaders of Lithuanian Jewry conferred in Mir, which then acquired the status of an autonomous community. From the second half of the 18th century, the economic situation of the community declined. In 1760, the Jews of Mir paid 480 zlotys in poll tax; the census of 1765 recorded 607 Jews in the town and vicinity who paid this tax.

Mir Yeshiva students in front of the Radziwill Castle in the town of Mir

---

3. Material for this section was adapted, in part, from "Mir," **Encyclopedia Judaica,** 1978 edition.

Prominent *rabbonim* officiated in Mir during the 18th century. The first *Av Bais Din* known by name (late 1720s) was Rabbi Meir ben Isaac Eisenstadt, followed by Rabbi Zev Hirsh HaKohen Rappaport. During the middle of the century, Rabbi Shlomo Zalman ben Yehuda Mirkish, author of **Shulchan Shlomo** (1771), held the position of Rov for 15 years. He was succeeded by Rabbi Zev Hirsh Eisenstadt. During the tenure of Rabbi Yosef Dovid Ajzensztat (1776-1826), the famous Mir Yeshiva was founded. At the beginning of the nineteenth century, Chabad Chasidim acquired considerable influence in the community.

In 1806 the Mir community numbered 807, including one hundred and six tailors, five goldsmiths, six cord makers, and about thirty other merchants. In the 65

YEAR	TAX	POPULATION
1673	45 Zlotys	—
1700	1,160 Zlotys	—
1720	1,350 Zlotys	—
1760	480 Zlotys	—
1765	—	607
1806	—	807
1847	—	2273
1897	—	3319
1921	—	2047

nearby villages there were 494 Jews in 1818. The number of Jews in Mir itself rose to 2,273 in 1847 and 3,319 (approximately 62% of the population) in 1897. From the second half of the nineteenth century, with the exception of the wood,

The Mirrer Yeshiva in Poland

grain, horse and textile merchants who formed the upper class, the majority of the local Jews were craftsmen such as *sofrim* and tailors and other occupations—carters and butchers.

The wooden synagogue built in the middle of the 18th century was burned down in 1901. This was followed by the constant threat of pogroms during the years of 1904-05. In 1921, there were 2,074 Jews in Mir, accounting for 55% of the population. Their difficult economic situation deteriorated even further in the late 1920s, a situation common throughout Poland at that time.

The yeshiva of Mir, founded by Rabbi Shmuel Chaim Tiktinski in 1815, and continued by his son Rabbi Avraham, played a central role in the spiritual life of Mir and the surrounding villages, and was an influence that spread throughout Eastern Europe. In the years before World War II students were attracted to the yeshiva from Eastern and Western Europe, including Germany and Belgium, and from as far away as America.

From 1836 the yeshiva was headed by Rabbi Moshe Avraham ben Yosef Ajensztat, and later by Rabbi Chaim Zalman Bresler. From 1880, the Rov of

In the years before World War II students were attracted to the yeshiva from Eastern and Western Europe, including Germany and Belgium, and from as far away as America.

THE MIRRER YESHIVA

Founded by Rabbi Shmuel Chaim Tiktinski: 1815
Rabbi Avrahom Tiktinski- Rosh HaYeshiva (son)
Rabbi Moshe ben Yosef Ajzensztat- Rosh HaYeshiva: 1836
Rabbi Chaim Leib Tiktinski- Rosh HaYeshiva: 1876
Rabbi Eliyahu Boruch Kamai- Rosh HaYeshiva: 1900
Rabbi Eliezer Yehuda Finkel- Rosh HaYeshiva: 1921(son-in-law of Rabbi Kamai)

ROSHEI HAYESHIVA OF MIR IN ERETZ YISRAEL:

Rabbi Eliezer Yehuda Finkel ZT"L: 1940
(Evacuated from Lithuania to Eretz Yisrael in 1940, reestablishing the Mirrer Yeshiva in Jerusalem.)

Rabbi Chaim Shmulevitz ZT"L: 1947
(Son-in-law of Rabbi Finkel ZT"L. Led the Mir to Japan and Shanghai with Rabbi Yechezkel Levenstein ZT"L.)

Rabbi Banish Finkel ZT"L: 1965

Rabbi Nochum Partzovitz ZT"L: 1967

Current (5756/1996):
Rabbi Nosson Tzvi Finkel, Shlita & Rabbi Rafael Shmulevitz, Shlita

ROSHEI HAYESHIVA OF MIR IN AMERICA:

Rabbi Avrahom Kalmanowitz ZT"L: 1947

Rabbi Ephraim Mordechai Ginsburg ZT"L: 1947

Current (5756/1996):
Rabbi Shmuel Berenbaum, Shlita & Rabbi Shraga Moshe Kalmanowitz, Shlita

the town was Rabbi Yom Tov Lipman. In 1903, he was followed by Rabbi Eliyahu Dovid Rabinowitz Tumim (known by the acronym "ADERET," father-in-law of Rav Avrahom Yitzchok Kook) who served until his *aliyah* to Eretz Yisrael. The last rabbi of Mir was Rabbi Avrahom Zev Kamai, who served in that position (and gave a *shiur* in the yeshiva) from 1917 until the Holocaust. During World War I the yeshiva moved to Poltava, but returned to Mir in 1921 when it was headed by Rabbi Eliezer Yehuda Finkel, son of the *Alter of Slabodka,* Rav Nosson Tzvi Finkel.

Rabbi Eliezer Yehuda Finkel

Rabbi Avrahom Kalmanowitz

Under Soviet rule (1939-1941) private enterprise was gradually stifled and factories, businesses and even large buildings were taken over by the state. The yeshiva's rabbis and students, led by Rabbi Finkel, evacuated to the city of Vilna in the still independent country of Lithuania. Through the efforts of Rabbi Avrahom Kalmanowitz, Rabbi Finkel managed to reach Palestine during the war, where he founded the Mir Yeshiva in Jerusalem. Most of the Mirrer Yeshiva was able to escape Nazi occupied Europe to Kobe, Japan, and finally to Shanghai, China, where they remained until the end of the war.

The Nazis captured Mir on June 27, 1941, and immediately executed scores of Jews on the charges of collaborating with the Russians. On November 9, 1941, 1,500 Jews were murdered on the outskirts of the town, with the remaining 850 Jews segregated into a ghetto. These survivors were transferred in May of 1942 to the ancient Mirski fortress located in the town.

On August 13th the final liquidation of the Jewish community of Mir was accomplished when those remaining in the Mirski fortress were murdered and buried in mass graves. Included in those killed after the German occupation of Mir were the yeshiva students and families who remained behind, along with the entire Jewish community who were not able to evade capture.

The Jewish community of Mir, like so many other communities throughout Eastern Europe, ceased to exist... men, women, children and babies all gave their lives *al Kiddush Hashem,* to sanctify the Name of Heaven.

The Jewish community of Mir, like so many other communities throughout Eastern Europe, ceased to exist... men, women, children and babies all gave their lives to sanctify the Name of Heaven.

TELZ

[Telz-Yiddish; Telsiai-Lithuanian; Telshi-Russian; Telschen-German]

PART I: *Historical Background* [4]

elz was an important Orthodox Jewish community situated in the Zamut Hills in Northwest Lithuania. Jews began populating Telz in the 17th century. In the latter part of the 19th century Telz was described as a politically conservative town that was very committed to Jewish tradition. The number of Jews living in Telz increased from 2,248 in 1847 to 4,204 in 1864. During the 1850's there were several years of famine in Lithuania, and the fact that Telz was somewhat isolated, without railroad connections, led to an economic decline and emigration from the town. In 1897 3,088 Jews lived in Telz, constituting 51% of the town.

After the German invasion of Lithuania, the Jewish community of Telz was completely destroyed. In July, 1941, all of the men were brutally tortured and killed by Lithuanian Fascists, and within six months all of the women were murdered as well. In 1970, the Jewish population of Telz was estimated at approximately 150 people.

PART II: *The Founding of the Yeshiva* [5]

Telz occupied a unique position among the Jewish communities of Eastern Europe due to the yeshiva that existed there from 1875 until 1941. The phenomenon that distinguished Telz from other yeshiva communities was that the Telzer Rov also occupied the position of Rosh HaYeshiva. Thus, the influence of the yeshiva permeated the town. Telz developed into a major center of Talmudic study under the guidance of Rabbi Eliezer Gordon, who held the position of Rov and Rosh Yeshiva from 1883 until 1910. Telz was literally a Torah town, with all policies of town management, including the regulation of commerce (pricing and profit margins, etc.)

Telz occupied a unique position among the Jewish communities of Eastern Europe due to the yeshiva that existed there from 1875 until 1941.

JEWISH POPULATION OF TELZ
1847 — 2,248
1864 — 4,204
1897 — 3,088 *(51% of population)*
Jewish Population destroyed by the Germans and Lithuanians: **July 1941—January 1942**
1970 — 150

---

4. The material for this section was adapted from "Telz" **Encyclopedia Judaica**, 1978 ed., pages 938-939.
5. Material for this section was taken from an interview with the Telzer Rosh HaYeshiva, Rabbi Mordecai Gifter, *Shlita,* and Rebbitzen Gifter, on 12/19/94. Additionally, material for this section, and the remaining sections of this essay, was adapted from: Surasky, Aharon; **Giants of Jewry,** (Chinuch Publications, Lakewood, N.J., 1982.)

under the direction of the Rosh Yeshiva. After the passing of Rabbi Gordon, his son-in-law Rabbi Yosef Leib Bloch took over the position of Rov and Rosh HaYeshiva from 1910 until 1930.

When Rabbi Gordon first arrived in Telz he found a gathering of exceptional scholars assembled seven years earlier by Rabbi Nosson Tzvi Finkel, The Alter of Slobodka and Rav Eliezer Yaakov Chvas, The Rov of Yanishok. This select group of *talmidim* was comprised of outstanding personalities such as Rav Meir Atlas (later Rov of Shavel), Rav Yaakov Tzvi Oppenheim (later Rov of Kelm), and Rav Shlomo Zalman Abel, the brother-in-law of Rabbi Shimon Shkop, Rosh Yeshiva of Grodna.

Rabbi Gordon introduced various innovations within the yeshiva system

Rabbi Eliezer Gordon

including a rigorous and novel approach to the study of *Talmud*, division of the yeshiva into five learning levels, administration of periodic tests to the *talmidim*, and compulsory attendance at all classes. In addition, he introduced *Mussar* (ethical and moral development) as a regular topic of study. Although the practice in other yeshivos was that the Rosh HaYeshiva delivered a general lecture before the entire yeshiva body, directed mainly at the older *talmidim*, Rabbi Gordon secured a singularly expert lecturer for each of the five levels so that each student would benefit from lectures given by their own

Rabbi Gordon introduced various innovations within the yeshiva system including a rigorous and novel approach to the study of Talmud.

Telz Yeshiva in Lithuania, pre-WWII

Maggid Shiur (lecturer). These lecturers were Torah giants such as Rabbi Shimon Shkop, Rabbi Chaim Rabinowitz, and the Rosh HaYeshiva's son-in-law, Rabbi Yosef Leib Bloch. The highest *shiur* was given by Rabbi Gordon himself.

An interesting episode took place when Rabbi Shimon Shkop left the yeshiva in 1903. Rabbi Gordon invited Rabbi Itzel Rabinowitz, the Rov of Ponevezh, one of the greatest scholars of the generation, to give a *shiur* in the yeshiva. Rabbi Gordon was immensely happy about Reb Itzel's acceptance. When Reb Itzel later changed his mind, Rabbi Gordon summoned him to a *Din Torah*, a Rabbinical Court, to settle the matter. He sent one of his students, Rabbi Yosef Shlomo Kahaneman (the future Ponevezher Rov who later built the Ponevezh Yeshiva in Bnei Brak) to represent the yeshiva at the court proceedings. After some discussion Rabbi Yosef Shlomo remarked to Rabbi Gordon that, although according to Talmudic law Rabbi Itzel is not allowed to retract, still he can send another in his place. To this Rabbi Gordon responded, "Another Reb Itzel? Is that possible? Does such a person exist?" This was the caliber of learning that Rabbi Gordon brought to Telz!

While the *shiurim* in most yeshivos were given at regular times with the students listening to the Rosh Yeshiva in silence, this was not true in Telz. As soon as Rabbi Gordon would begin his *shiur* one student would ask a question, another would suggest an

Rabbi Yitzchok Yaakov Rabinowitz (R' Itzel Ponevezher)

Rabbi Yosef Kahaneman (the Ponevezher Rov)

answer, a third would bring a proof, while yet another would bring another proof to disprove the entire argument. Rabbi Gordon, mind and eyes flashing, would join in the give-and-take, raising the intensity level of the learning to greater heights.

During the summer months Rabbi Gordon's *shiur* was set for 4:00pm. During the winter, when the days were shorter, the Rosh Yeshiva's *shiur* was given at 4:00am. While the town of Telz slept, the Rosh Yeshiva's home was throbbing with the learning of Torah.

Even though the yeshiva was divided into five different levels, the Rosh Yeshiva still gave a general *shiur* to the whole yeshiva one day a week, a day of true battling for the sake of Torah. The students would furiously debate the topic with the Rosh Yeshiva, and he would storm back against their arguments. At times he would leave the *bimah* to walk amongst the students and debate with them, point-for-point, like an equal within the group. One day the students agreed not to interrupt the *shiur*. After several minutes of lecturing in silence, Rabbi Gordon descended from the *bimah* commenting that he was not prepared to give his *shiur* in a cemetery.

PART III: *The Rov and the Town* [6]

Rabbi Gordon was concerned with every aspect of communal life in Telz, and nothing was done without his involve-

During the winter, when the days were shorter, the Rosh Yeshiva's shiur was given at 4:00 am. While the town of Telz slept, the Rosh Yeshiva's home was throbbing with the learning of Torah.

ment. After a protracted dispute with the district governor, the revenue from the meat tax collected from the Jews of Telz, usually spent on churches and gentile schools, was directed instead for the building of *mikvaos* and the maintenance of the city's synagogues. Other such examples of Rabbi Gordon's involvement in the city affairs are recorded in the following three incidents:

1. *Baron Kayserling, a well-known Russian nobleman, once leased a dairy which had been run by a Jewish tenant for many years to a new Jewish dairyman. The former tenant called the encroacher to a* Din Torah, *and when the latter refused to appear, Rabbi Eliezer proclaimed a* cherem *on the products of the dairyman. The enraged Baron demanded that the Rov cease to interfere in his affairs, and punctuated his demands with threats. But Rabbi Eliezer retorted sharply that the deciding factor in his eyes was Torah law and that no threat could make him retract his position. The Baron yielded and put the dairy back into the hands of the original tenant. The Baron claimed he had consulted with the mayor of Kovno, who advised him not to become embroiled in a quarrel with the Rov of Telz since the Rov could not be swayed by threats or sweet talk.*

2. *When it came to Rabbi Eliezer's attention that the storekeepers were using inexact weights and measures, Rabbi Eliezer ordered the storekeepers to switch all their measures to new ones, and be as exacting in weighing items for gentiles as for Jews. The Rov himself went to the marketplace to see that his ruling was carried out. This ruling became known throughout the surrounding region, even among the gentiles, and when they came to Telz to shop, they demanded that the storekeepers use "the Rabbi's weights and measures."*

3. *In those days, it was customary for the matzoh factories to employ men, women and even young children throughout most the of the night. Rabbi Eliezer gave strict orders that the bakeries in Telz be closed no later than 11 pm. His official reason was that if the workers were tired they would not be able to maintain the meticulous* kashruth *necessary for matzoh production. However, to his close friends he revealed that his purpose was to protect the workers from exploitation and overwork. Rabbi Eliezer enforced this regulation stringently. If any bakery owner disobeyed it, the Rov ordered the* mashgichim *to declare the dough in that bakery* chametz.

Rabbi Gordon and the Maskilim

Rabbi Gordon fought relentlessly against the reforms of the *maskilim* (adherents to the Enlightenment Movement). He attempted to publish an Orthodox newspaper that would serve as a vehicle for counteracting the many publications written by the reformers. The Rov founded the first religious Jewish organization in Russia, *Knesses Yisrael*, and was active in establishing branches of *Knesses Yisrael* in every city and village. The Rov was a participating founder in the worldwide Agudath Israel movement, and attended the first congress held in Hamburg. In a letter to Rabbi Yitzchok Blauser in 1907, Rabbi Gordon expressed his sadness that, "the magnitude of atheism which has spread among our nation's youth is unimaginable, and every day we see boys and girls who were yesterday united with G-d and His Torah transformed into heretics."

Rabbi Gordon's fight against the reformers did not go unnoticed by his adversaries. They denounced his yeshiva to the Russian government and maligned

The Rov was a participating founder in the worldwide Agudath Israel movement, and attended the first congress held in Hamburg.

When it came to Rabbi Eliezer's attention that the storekeepers were using inexact weights and measures, Rabbi Eliezer ordered the storekeepers to switch all their measures to new ones.

the yeshiva in their periodicals, *Hameilitz* and *Hatzofeh*. The reformers demanded that the fund-raisers for Telz Yeshiva not be allowed in any community to collect funds since the Rosh Yeshiva, Rabbi Eliezer Gordon, was not a true Russian patriot.

At one point the *maskilim* reported the illegal Telz Yeshiva (the Russian government had not allowed the yeshiva to exist legally) to the Mayor of Kovno. An inspector arrived, found a full *Beis Hamedrash*, and began writing his report. Rabbi Gordon signaled for the *talmidim* to start leaving one at a time, until there were only twenty students left. Rabbi Gordon approached the inspector and asked to read his report. Upon seeing that he wrote there were hundreds of students the Rov asked the inspector if it was proper to lie in such a report when, in fact, there were not more than twenty or so students present. After counting the *talmidim* with Rabbi Gordon, the inspector conceded that the Rov was correct. Since there were not more then twenty students the place could not be considered a yeshiva, and the inspector discarded his report. He went back to Kovno with a nice tip and reported to the Mayor that there was no yeshiva in Telz.

Soon after a new Mayor by the name of Popov was appointed. Popov was evil, hated Jews, and was not susceptible to bribery. As soon as he was installed, he summoned Rabbi Eliezer and warned

Rabbi Yosef Leib Bloch

him that if he did not stop teaching in the yeshiva, the Rov would be deported from Telz—perhaps to Siberia. Rov Eliezer answered him calmly, "I am not afraid of you, for even if I am exiled to Siberia, I will have a yeshiva there, too. But I would advise you to desist from your designs, for if you are banished, it is extremely doubtful whether you will be appointed district ruler in your exile." Indeed, it was not long before Popov was dismissed from office.[7]

The Lineage of Telz

After the passing of Rabbi Eliezer Gordon, his son-in-law, Rabbi Yosef Leib Bloch, assumed the mantle of the leadership of the yeshiva. Under Rabbi Yosef Leib the yeshiva continued to flourish, becoming one of the largest in all of Europe. In addition to counteracting the government's modern educational institutions for Jews which were built to compete with the traditional *cheder* and yeshiva system, Rabbi Yosef Leib began his own modern Talmud Torah where children could study Torah and secular studies under licensed teachers (as required by the government). The Rov made sure that the Talmud Torah was a state of the art institution that could easily challenge the German-style secular schools. The Rov charged his sons, Rabbi Avrohom Yitzchok (future Rov and Rosh HaYeshiva) and Rabbi Eliyohu Meir (founder of Telz, Cleveland) to head the Talmud Torah, admonishing them to be well aware of the great and holy function such a school would play in keeping Jewish youth from falling into the hands of the *maskilim*.

In addition, Rabbi Yosef Leib started Yavne, a preparatory girls' high school, including secular studies. This program came

Under Rabbi Yosef Leib (Bloch) the yeshiva continued to flourish, becoming one of the largest in all of Europe.

---

7. Surasky, Aharon; pages 80-82

under great criticism from many *rabbonim.* However, the sainted Chofetz Chaim supported Rabbi Bloch, declaring that he felt that Rabbi Yosef Leib was well aware of his actions and had certainly proceeded with great *deliberation.* These actions were to have great future consequences for the yeshiva, because afterwards the Lithuanian government ordered that all yeshivos must have secular studies or lose their status

as theological institutes whose students were exempt from the military draft. Finally, Rabbi Bloch started the first teacher training school for religious teachers and a seminary for women.

The End of Telz in Lithuania

When the Nazis reached Telz they recruited local Lithuanian anti-Semites to help them carry out their plans for the final

THE TELZ DYNASTY		
Founded in 1885 by Rabbi Eliezer Gordon		
Rabbi Eliezer Gordon	Rov and Rosh HaYeshiva	1841-1910
Rabbi Yosef Leib Bloch (son-in-law of Rabbi Gordon)	Rov and Rosh HaYeshiva	1860-1929
Rabbi Avrohom Yitzchok Bloch (Son of Rabbi Y.L. Bloch)	Rov and Rosh HaYeshiva	Killed by Nazis in 1941. He led the yeshiva and community in giving their lives al *Kiddush Hashem.*
Rabbi Zalman Bloch (Son of Rabbi Y.L. Bloch)	Menahel Ruchoni	Killed al *Kiddush Hashem,* 1941
Rabbi Eliyohu Meir Bloch (Son of Rabbi Y.L. Bloch)	Co-founder of Telz, Cleveland	Died, 1955
Rabbi Chaim Mordechai Katz (Son-in-law of Rabbi Y.L. Bloch)	Co-founder of Telz, Cleveland	Died, 1965
Rabbi Boruch Sorotzkin (son-in-law of Rabbi A.Y. Bloch, and son of Rabbi Zalman Sorotzkin, son-in-law of Rabbi Eliezer Gordon)	Rosh HaYeshiva, Telz, Cleveland	1917-1979
Rabbi Mordecai Gifter (Son-in-law of Rabbi Zalman Bloch)	Rosh HaYeshiva, Telz, Cleveland	
Rabbi Chaim Stein Rabbi Aizik Ausband (son-in-law of Rabbi A.Y. Bloch) Rabbi Pesach Stein (Son-in-law of Rabbi Zalman Bloch)	Roshei Yeshiva, Telz, Cleveland	

The Rosh
HaYeshiva,
*Rabbi Avrohom
Yitzchok Bloch,
led his yeshiva
and community in
the sanctification
of Hashem's Name.*

solution of the Jews of Telz. The Rosh HaYeshiva, Rabbi Avrohom Yitzchok Bloch, led his yeshiva and community in the sanctification of Hashem's Name. Refusing the chance to flee to safety in Russia, Rabbi Bloch remained in Telz to give courage and strength to his fellow Jews. His daughter, Rebbetzin Chaya Ausband, witnessed Rabbi Bloch's final hours:

> *When the German troops rounded up the entire Jewish population and lined them up facing their bayonets, Father did not recoil from their shouts and threats. With absolute serenity he addressed the community, exhorting them to repent and accept upon themselves the yoke of Heaven. He inspired them all to the exalted heights of being willing to be sacrificed for the sanctification of Hashem. During the last moments he requested water to wash his hands and, from inside the mass grave that the Jews had been forced to dig for themselves, his voice burst forth in a cry of "Shema Yisroel" in sanctity and purity.*[8]

Rabbi Eliyohu Meir Bloch and his brother-in-law, Rabbi Chaim Mordechai Katz, escaped from Telz just before its destruction by the Nazis. Traveling through Siberia and Japan, they eventually arrived in Cleve-

8. Surasky, Aharon; page 292.

land where they began rebuilding the Telz Yeshiva and continued its tradition. They founded a day school, a high school and teachers' seminary.

In 1955, with the passing of their illustrious uncle, Rabbi Eliyohu Meir Bloch—

Rabbi Boruch Sorotzkin and Rabbi Mordecai Gifter, Shlita, were called upon to serve as Roshei Yeshiva of Telz, Cleveland, with Rabbi Chaim Mordechai Katz. With the passing

Rabbi Boruch Sorotzkin

of Rabbi Katz in 1965, they served together as Roshei HaYeshiva until Reb Boruch's passing in 1979. Rabbi Sorotzkin, one of the leading Torah personalities of his day, perpetuated the legacy of Telz, Lithuania, on American shores. Rabbi Sorotzkin was one of the main builders of the Hebrew Academy of Cleveland, serving as the Chairman of the Academy's Vaad HaChinuch from 1965. He was the Academy's mainstay in all matters—spiritual and material. Reb Boruch's spiritual imprint is deeply embedded within the accomplishments of the Academy and in its many *Talmidim*.

*Telz Yeshiva in
Cleveland, Ohio
today*

≋ VILNA

[Wilno-Polish; Vilnius-Lithuanian]

PART I: *Historical Background* [9]

ilna has been the capital of the grand duchy of Lithuania since 1323. In 1527 King Sigismund I issued a declaration forbidding Jews from settling in Vilna. In 1551, two Jews were given permission to reside and do business in Vilna. The first recorded information regarding an organized Jewish community in Vilna dates from 1568, when the Jews were ordered to pay the poll tax. Tradition has it that a wooden synagogue was built in Vilna in 1573.

In 1592, the street where the synagogue was located was officially named Jew's Street. In that year a mob ransacked the houses and shops of the Jewish community, as well as the synagogue itself.

In 1593, Sigismund II reissued permission for Jews to reside and do business in Vilna. The Jews of Vilna were given a charter of privileges in February, 1633. This charter allowed them to engage in all branches of commerce, distilling, and any crafts not protected by guilds (an early form of labor unions). Jews were still restricted in where they could live, but they were allowed to build a new synagogue, this time of stone. Only 12 Jewish shops could have openings facing the streets. Shops could be leased for no more than 10 years. An annual tax of 300 zlotys in peacetime, and 500 zlotys in wartime was placed upon the community.

In 1634 and 1635, the community was again plundered by marauders. Ladislaus IV commissioned an investigation into these acts of violence and ordered the city to protect its Jewish citizens and compensate for the damages sustained. Jesuit academy students instigated further acts of violence in 1639 and 1641.

During the first half of the 17th century, Vilna experienced significant growth. Jews arrived from Prague, Frankfort and various Polish towns. Among these Jews were scholars and men of significant wealth. At this time in Vilna there were approxi-

In 1592, the street where the synagogue was located was officially named Jew's Street. In that year a mob ransacked the houses and shops of the Jewish community, as well as the synagogue itself.

Panorama of Vilna on the Wilia River

mately 3,000 Jewish residents out of a total population of 15,000 citizens.

In 1630, Vilna suffered from a general economic deterioration that affected most of Lithuania's Jews. The commu-

---

9. Material for this section was taken from "Vilna," **Encyclopedia Judaica,** 1978 Ed.

nity received help in alleviating some of this economic distress by being allowed to undertake business in "all the townlets, villages, boroughs, and settlements" under the jurisdiction of other major communities in Lithuania. In 1648-1649, the community readily gave aid to the suffering fugitives of the Chmielnicki massacres, thus placing further economic hardship upon themselves.

In 1652, Vilna was given the title of *Kehillah Rosh Bais Din,* Community Head of the Courts, and in 1661 was established as the seat of leadership for all of Lithuanian Jewry. Hostility between the Jews and the gentile townspeople continued under the instigation of the Jesuits. A riot in 1687, promoted by Jesuit students, included gentile artisans and shopkeepers. The apparent reason for the riot was to force the Jews to drop payment on debts owed them. The community suffered 120,000 zlotys worth of damage. King John Sobieski severely admonished the city for the violence and disallowed the forgiving of any debts owed to the Jews by the city residents. By 1690, there were 227 Jewish families living in Vilna and an equal amount in the surrounding areas, a population somewhat less than the 3,000 living in Vilna in the first half of the century. It is probable that many Jews moved to other towns and cities due to the violence and economic hardship they encountered in Vilna.

The Northern War (1700-1721)[10] with Sweden brought great economic hardship on the community. High taxes were levied on the Jews of Vilna who sought some financial relief by pawning their ritual objects with their gentile neighbors. Famine and plague also took their toll. When the Jewish quarter burned in 1737, Amsterdam Jews responded generously.

Throughout the first three quarters of the 18th century the Jews of Vilna continued to struggle with their gentile neighbors for the right to live and conduct business in an unrestricted atmosphere. Living and business rights granted one year would be replaced the next year with more stringent restrictions or unfair compromises. The Jews even faced expulsion at times. Finally in 1783, restrictions on occupations and residence (except for two streets) were lifted. Jews were now obligated to pay the same taxes as the general population. When the Russians conquered the city after the Lithuania uprising in 1794, the station of the Jews continued to improve. The Russians eliminated municipal court jurisdiction over the Jews, restoring to the community autonomy over its internal affairs. The Jewish population in Vilna during the 1795 census recorded 3,613 Jews in Vilna and the surrounding areas.

PART II: *The Jerusalem of Lithuania*

By the beginning of the 17th century Vilna had become an important center of Talmudic studies. The first report of a Talmud Torah program was recorded in the second half of the century. Famous sages born in Vilna from the beginning of the century (and into the 18th century in chronological order) include: Rabbi Yehoshua Hoeschel ben Yosef; Rabbi Shabbetai haKohen, a city *dayan* (rabbinical judge); Rabbi Moshe ben Yitzchak Yehuda

By the beginning of the 17th Century Vilna had become an important center of Talmudic studies. The first report of a Talmud Torah program was recorded in the second half of the century.

---

10. The Northern War was a general conflict that involved most of the countries on the European continent. It started chiefly from the desire of the neighbors of Sweden to break Swedish supremacy in the Baltic Sea area, and from the various ambitions of Peter I of Russia and Charles XII of Sweden. The lasting results of the war were the waning of Swedish power, the establishment of Russia as a major power of Europe and the decay of Poland.

Lima, Rov of the city in mid-century; Rabbi Moshe, a forbearer of the Vilna Gaon; Rabbi Moshe's son-in-law Yosef, author of *Rosh Yosef;* Rabbi Baruch Kahana, known as Baruch Charif; Azriel the grammarian and his two sons, Nissan and Eliyohu; Zevi Hirsch Kaidanover; and Yekuthiel Gordon, a physician who had studied in Padua, Italy, and had come under the influence of the holy Rabbi Moshe Chaim Luzatto, author of the *sefer Mesillas Yesharim* (Pathway of the Just).

The second half of the 18th century was dominated by the personality and scholarship of Rabbi Eliyahu ben Solomon Zalman, the sainted "Vilna Gaon," whose Torah and saintliness had a lasting influence on Torah Jewry throughout the world, and in Eretz Yisrael in particluar. The Gaon's influence transformed Vilna into a center of Torah and piety, with significant influence on the study of *halacha* and *kabalah.* Vilna became the focal point for the life-style and studies of the *Misnagdim.* Opposition to the new *Chassidic* style of worship and study in Vilna was very great, particularly from the year 1772, until 1802. An overall accommodation between the two groups was only reached after both sides sought intervention from the Russian government between 1795 and 1798.

The Jewish population in Vilna in 1800 was 6,917. At that point the Jews requested the right to be involved in communal affairs, and though permission was granted, these plans were frustrated by the general population.

During the war with Napoleon in 1812, the Jews remained loyal to Russia, despite their grievances and sufferings. When the French provincial government was set up in Vilna, Jews were heavily taxed. French troops desecrated the Jewish cemetery and used it as a cattle pen. Rights for involvement in communal affairs that were granted under the rule of Czar Nicholas I were canceled, and the community's autonomy over its internal affairs was abolished in 1844. From then on, the *gabbaim* of the *tzedakah* fund unofficially guided the affairs of the community.

Tomb of the Vilna Gaon (1720-1797)

The Enlightenment

Throughout this period, Talmudic learning in Vilna flourished. Members of the *Haskalah* (Enlightenment) noted the success of Torah study in Vilna and decided to become active as well. When the government russification of the Jews began, *Haskalah* members chose Vilna as the center of their activites. Modern Enlightenment schools were set up, and in 1847 a government sponsored rabbinical seminary was founded. *Maskilim* who once used these schools to glorify the Polish language and culture, now put all their effort into the glorification of Russian language

The second half of the 18th century was dominated by the personality and scholarship of Rabbi Eliyahu ben Solomon Zalman, the sainted "Vilna Gaon."

and culture. The Torah community suffered greatly from the anti-Jewish propaganda of an apostate named Jacob Brafmann and from the anti-religious works of the *maskilim* and their weekly publication, *Ha-Carmel*. It was at this time that the first Jewish Socialists began to infiltrate the running of the "official" rabbinical seminary in Vilna.

Anti-Jewish riots in 1881 were prevented by the Jewish butchers, who organized to oppose the rioters and turned them over to the police. Due to the Russian government's policy of forbidding Jews to live in the outlying villages, many Jews moved into Vilna, causing congestion and increased unemployment. The number of Jews living in Vilna in 1897 was 63,831. At this time many Jews emigrated to the United States and South Africa.

Vilna's Torah community came under further attack in the 1890s when the city became the center of activities for Jewish Socialists, Jewish Social Democrats and the Bund Labor Party. Ultimately, at the beginning of the 20th century Vilna became the headquarters of the secular Zionist Movement in Russia and the center for activities celebrating Hebrew and Yiddish literature. In 1921, there were approximately 46,500 Jews living in Vilna (36% of the overall population), and in 1931 there were approximately 55,000 in Vilna (28% of the population).

PART III:
The Vilna Experience— Rabbi Chaim Ozer Grodzenski From 1896 to 1940

The Orthodox community was under the leadership of Rabbi Chaim Ozer Grodzenski, and closely associated with

Rabbi Eliezer Silver, trapped in Europe on a visit to his parents during the war, observed that in one instance Reb Chaim Ozer secured food and lodging for over two thousand refugees within several hours.

Agudath Israel. During World War I, over 600,000 Jewish men went to war for "mother" Russia.[11] Those not drafted were expected to do whatever necessary to support the war effort. When train loads of soldiers passed through Vilna on their way

Rabbi Chaim Ozer Grodzenski

to the front, Jewish women and girls waited at the station with milk and food, while yeshiva students helped the wounded to ambulances.

When the war effort floundered, Jews from the western provinces of Russia were ordered to evacuate, and thousands of Jews from Kovno, Grodno and Suvalk poured into Vilna. Under the leadership of Reb Chaim Ozer the citizenry of Vilna rose to meet the challenges of taking care of this tidal wave of refugees. Rabbi Eliezer Silver, trapped in Europe on a visit to his parents during the war, observed that in one instance Reb Chaim Ozer secured food and lodging for over two thousand refugees within several hours.

The following episode, personally witnessed by Rabbi Yehuda Leib Graubart and recorded in his **Sefer Zikaron,** conveys the terror that the Jewish population lived

---

11. Material for this section was adapted from, Shimon Finkelman, **Reb Chaim Ozer, The Life and Ideals of Rabbi Chaim Ozer Grodzenski of Vilna** (ArtScroll, New York, 1987).

through at the hands of their Russian countrymen during the First World War.

It was late afternoon on Yom Kippur in the town of Stachuv and the Jews were crowded in their shul tearfully reciting the Neilah *prayer. The town had already been the scene of a pogrom and its Jewish-owned stores were being looted regularly by the regiments that occupied the town. Suddenly, a child ran into the* shul *shouting that a Jew was hanging in the street. The congregants dashed out and were met by the sight of a lifeless body dangling from a lamppost. They recognized the victim as a Jew from neighboring Shatsigan.*

As I, the local Rov, ran about frantically trying to discover what had led to the hanging, I was met by a gentile who informed me that a Cossack band had just murdered ten Jews on the outskirts of the town.

That night, a widow of one of the victims related what had happened. The previous night, the eve of Yom Kippur, the house of a gentile farmer in Shatsigan caught fire. The next morning, the farmer's wife went to the Stachuv hospital to procure salve for the burns on her hands. While in Stachuv she met a shoemaker to whom she recounted her ordeal. The shoemaker asked if she suspected arson, to which she replied in the negative. The shoemaker countered, "aren't there any Jews in Shatsigan? For sure one of them set fire to your house!" The woman did not need much convincing and she began to think which Jew might have a personal grudge against her family. She recalled that two weeks previously, she had gleefully accompanied some Cossacks when they looted a Jewish store. The shoemaker said that, without a doubt, the storekeeper was the arsonist; they soon were standing be-

fore the army commandant, accusing the Jew of a crime he knew nothing about.

The soldiers did not find their man in Shatsigan proper. He, along with some of his Jewish neighbors, were spending the Holy Day in a small shul on the outskirts of the town. By the time the fire in the farmer's house had broken out, the storekeeper had already donned his kittel, *wrapped himself in his* tallis *and was praying the* Ma'ariv *service. After the prayers had ended, the storekeeper and ten other men remained in the* shul *to recite* Tehillim *through the night.*

The soldiers rounded up the eleven men and brought them to the commandant. It took less than five minutes to decide the fate of those innocent souls. The 'arsonist' was to be hung in public for all to see and take heed of, while the others would be disposed of out of sight.
(Finkelman, Shimon, pages 71-72.)

This Russian commandant, like so many other anti-Semites, ignored his own deplorable state to focus his energy and resources on the destruction of the Jews. Years later the Nazis would use this same warped reasoning. They too would commandeer valuable trains, monies, supplies and personnel to the fulfillment of their dream to destroy the Jews, even though they were losing the war on two fronts. This was the irrational hatred and treachery of the gentiles with which the Jews of Eastern Europe lived for over two thousand years.

For four years, from 1915 until 1919, Reb Chaim Ozer was forced to flee from Vilna because the retreating Russian

Yet even in exile, Reb Chaim Ozer continued his efforts to raise funds for the yeshivas that were forced to flee.

A woman reading from the "Tzene Rene" in Vilna.

Poor living conditions in Eastern Europe during World War I

Army contemplated taking the leaders of the Vilna community as political prisoners and sentencing them to slave labor. Yet even in exile, Reb Chaim Ozer continued his efforts to raise funds for the yeshivas that were forced to flee deep into the heartland of Russia, and for the wandering souls who sought refuge in far away towns and villages that had no yeshivas, Talmud Torahs, *mikvaos*, or kosher *shechita*. Thousands of letters were written and thousands of prayers were offered from the hand and heart of this spiritual giant who felt the pain and woe of the Jewish people in this time of turmoil and exile.

Under Reb Chaim Ozer's leadership and inspiration shuls, *chadarim*, yeshivas and *mikvaos* were founded in scores of cities and towns. He provided each com-

munity with a *shochet* and Torah instructors for the children, along with their monthly salaries. He oversaw the curriculum of the *chadarim* and was consulted in their day to day affairs. He procured *siddurim, chumashim*, and *gemaros, tefillin, mezuzos* and *Sifrei Torah*. All this was accomplished without the personnel and organizational apparatus one would normally associate with such large endeavors.

Reb Chaim Ozer was spiritual guide, project coordinator, administrator and fundraiser all in one. The last role was perhaps the hardest of all for him, since his weak constitution was not suited to frequent excursions. Still, he traveled near and far in search of funds. Reb Chaim Ozer's stature and the magnetic charm of his personality secured cordial receptions wherever he went. His personal appeals in Kiev,

Moscow and other cities were well received."[12]

Spiritual Holocaust

Through a thousand years of exile in Europe and Asia, through persecutions, expulsions and massacres, **never** was there any significant deviation from complete and uncompromising Jewish loyalty to the Torah. Under living conditions that included exposure to rain, snow and cold, discriminatory laws that barely allowed a Jew to earn a living and open animosity of Church and state, Jews remained steadfast in their beliefs. While during this time an individual or family may have left Judaism, it was not until the nineteenth century, and the advent of the *Haskala* (Enlightenment), that this situation radically changed.

The estrangement from Torah that began with the spirit of Napoleon's Emancipation, and advanced under the banner of the Enlightenment, fragmented the Jewish nation in the 1880s into distinct camps: the Orthodox, Torah true Jewry on the one side, with the various political and/or cultural groups whose ideologies were meant to replace Torah on the other. The Jews who abandoned Torah put their hopes in movements like Socialism, Bundism and Zionism. These Jews sought to impress their views on all of Vilna's Jewry. They used the upheaval of WWI to acquire key communal positions which allowed them control of relief funds. They used these funds to open secular elementary schools in areas where such educational institutions for Jewish youth had never existed. Reb Chaim Ozer addresses the severity and tragedy of this issue in the following

left to right: Rabbi Chizkiyah Mishkowsky, Rabbi Zalman Sorotzkin and Reb Chaim Ozer

letter dealing with funds from abroad for the re-establishment of Lithuanian Torah institutions:

What we never imagined seeing has occurred. A great upheaval has taken place in but a short period of time. The frightful days of war arrived and cast the entire world into turmoil. The expulsions began, the decrees and wanderings in Zamut and Lithuania, along with the departure of all the yeshivas from those places. Then came the German occupation with all its consequences and effects (see chapter).

Upon my return to Lithuania, I was astonished to see the two-fold blow it had been dealt—both its material and spiritual foundations have been destroyed. The spiritual devastation exceeds the material one; the greater an object's sanctity, the greater its devastation.

> Through a thousand years of exile in Europe and Asia, through persecutions, expulsions and massacres, **never** was there any significant deviation from complete and uncompromising Jewish loyalty to the Torah.

---

12. Ibid., page 75. The student is urged to read the pertinent chapters for a full accounting of the hardships and persecution the Jews of Vilna and Poland faced under the conflicting armies during World War I.

Battei Midrash *are desolate and in the* chadarim *there is dread and fear. There are no functioning* chadarim *even for young children. In Vilna, the situation is depressing...The* chadarim *have been replaced by schools, most of which teach that Torah is merely a matter of language, and need not be internalized. In some of these schools, the primary goal is to uproot what has been planted and to cause all of Torah and mitzvos to be forgotten—relegating Torah to a level of fables and legends, G-d forbid."[13]*

Children in Vilna going to the Mefitzei Haskalah school in 1929

In another part of this letter Reb Chaim Ozer describes the eternity of Torah and its adherents as follows:

"... Through the course of our people's history, our enemies from within and without have attempted to seal off the purifying waters of Israel and thought that they would succeed at uprooting Israel and its Torah. But they were mistaken. The Torah of Israel is not a cistern of still water; rather, it is a flowing spring that, when blocked on its sides,

will channel a path for itself from beneath and suddenly gush upward from other ground so that its waters may rise to give life to multitudes..."[14]

The Second World War

Vilna, originally the capital of Lithuania, was seized by Poland after World War I. From then on, a state of war existed between Poland and Lithuania. Kovno became Lithuania's temporary capital. On October 10, 1939 Russia announced that it would return Vilna to Lithuania as part of a "mutual defense treaty" which permitted Soviet military bases inside Lithuania. The Lithuanian government, as surprised as anyone by the move, greeted it with both joy and wariness. On the one hand, they were ecstatic to have their ancient capital back. Still, they knew the implications of giving the Russians a foothold in their country. However, they had no alternative, for the Russians coerced them into signing the treaty.

On October 7, three days before the above announcement was made, Reb Chaim Ozer telegraphed a number of *Roshei Yeshiva* to come to Vilna for an urgent meeting. He had learned of Vilna's imminent change of government. Until the city did change hands, its borders with Poland would still be open. This meant that the yeshivas of eastern Poland had a brief opportunity to head for Vilna and re-establish themselves there, under a Lithuanian regime that would permit them to function. Reb Chaim Ozer realized that it would be only a matter of time before Lithuania was absorbed by Russia or Germany, but meanwhile there would be time for Jews to try to escape to the free world. Reb Chaim Ozer

---

13. Ibid., pages 84-85
14. Ibid., page 86.

The Meatmarket Street located in the old Jewish quarter in Vilna

Entrance to Vilna's Jewish Quarter

Roman Vishniac

assumed responsibility for the support of the Torah army that was to gather under his wings.[15]

More than 20,000 refugees entered Vilna before the political situation changed—among them there were 2,500 yeshiva students and *rebbaim*.

The refugees, including the yeshiva students, traveled to Vilna any way they could— by train, car, wagon or on foot. The roads were fraught with danger; military roadblocks forced groups of students to scatter. Most managed to arrive at their destination. The yeshivas of Mir, Kletzk, Radin, Kamenitz, Baranovich, and Bialystok arrived in Vilna virtually intact. Others, such as Grodno, Volozhin, Lomza, Lutsk and Novardok were among those that arrived only in part. Some suggested that the fragmented yeshivas combine

15. Ibid., page 224.

for the sake of space and other practicalities. Reb Chaim Ozer disagreed and asserted that each yeshiva should maintain its own unique identity. This applied also to the Chassidic yeshivas of Lublin, Lubavitch, Slonim and Mezritch, parts of which had found their way to the city. Even when some of the *talmidim* of Yeshiva Chachmei Lublin asked to become part of the Mirrer yeshiva, Reb Chaim Ozer refused to grant their request. No yeshiva should be allowed to dissolve, he held, especially one as renowned as Lublin.[16]

---

16. Ibid., page 225. The student is referred to the chapter "Captain in the Storm" for material regarding refugee life in Vilna and the eventual expulsion of the yeshivas from Vilna . See page 140 at the end of this section for other comprehensive sources of Orthodox rescue efforts during WW II.

Meeting With History: Jewish Life in Poland and Lithuania

The spiritual and material life of Torah Jewry from 1900
until the beginning of World War II, September 1, 1939,
as retold through the life experiences of:

The Telzer Rosh HaYeshiva,
Rabbi Mordecai Gifter, *Shlita,* and Rebbetzin S. Gifter
(Interview conducted 12/19/94)

The Rosh HaYeshiva, Bais Yisroel Torah Center
Rabbi Avigdor Miller, *Shlita*
(Interview conducted 6/12/96)

The Founder and Dean of the Hebrew Academy of Cleveland,
Rabbi Nochum Zev Dessler, *Shlita*
(Interview conducted 12/19/94)

and

Rebbetzin Zlota Ginsburg
daughter of Rabbi Yechezkel Levenstein, *ZT"L*
(Interview conducted during the months of June and July, 1994)

Roman Vishniac

REFLECTIONS ON TELZ AND LITHUANIAN TORAH LIFE:

Remembrances of the Telz Rosh HaYeshiva, Rabbi Mordecai Gifter, Shlita and Rebbetzin Shoshana Gifter

"Telz was a royal realm of Torah where everything was under the control of the Yeshiva. The Rosh HaYeshiva also served as Rov of the town, so nothing took place in Telz without the consent of the Rosh HaYeshiva. The policy of the Jewish bank, the administration of Yavne (the school for girls), the *Yeshiva K'tana* for boys and the summer camp for poor children were all under the control of the Yeshiva. There was even a Jewish hospital that was built and administered under the direction of the Rosh HaYeshiva.

This is something you fail to see in life in America, that Torah is the sole criteria governing all aspects of the life of the individual and the community. In most of *Galus* we see that Jews have been forced to bear the yoke of secular law (not often was it as accommodating to the religious Jew as is American civil law), and often were ruled by the religious law of the countries where they resided. Even in America much of American law is in conflict with Torah. A Jew lives in a fragmented society in *Galus*. In Telz, however, everything was Torah Law, and the Rosh HaYeshiva directed all the activities of the community according to the strict dictates of the Torah.

Rabbi Yosef Leib Bloch, Rov and Rosh HaYeshiva of Telz, initiated a number of revolutionary projects. He started the Yavne school for girls, because he saw that girls needed an education to build a proper Jewish home. In addition, he viewed such a school as a fortress against the teachings of the Enlightenment. The school had a full curriculum including the expectation that the girls become proficient in Hebrew. Sara Schenirer founded the Bais Yaakov Teacher's Seminary after Yavne was already established. Bais Yaakov was in Poland, and Telz was in Lithuania; and since there wasn't peace between the two countries it was very difficult for the girls in Lita (Lithuania) to get into Poland to attend the Bais Yaakov schools. For a long time the only school for girls in Lithuania was Yavne. Reb Yosef Leib also started a seminary for teachers so there would be trained *melamdim* and *moros* to teach throughout Eastern Europe. All of this was before WWI.

Rabbi Bloch was a global person, a person who thought about the welfare of *Klal Yisrael*. He taught that one must think about how to strengthen Torah within the local community and throughout the world—he saw the continuity of *Klal Yisrael* in what he did.

As soon as you entered the Telz town limits you were already in the *Beis Hamedrash*, because everything that took place in town was according to the teachings of the Yeshiva. There was a Rabbi Meisels who ran a little grocery store. He had a large family and was very poor. When you came to buy something he would tell you to shop by Reb Mendel, another grocer, because he sold the same item a penny cheaper. "You can pay a penny less by Reb Mendel," he would say. "I can't afford to sell it cheaper because I don't have such a big store. So, maybe you'll shop over there." He was called the Tzaddik of Telz, and he was a grocer. You see what a person can become in such an environment. Because he was so honest, Rabbi Meisels was put in charge of all the *gemachs* (Free Loan Societies) in the town. He was so poor he had almost nothing for his family, but he was in charge of all of the *gemach* monies.

The yeshiva was our home and we felt that it was where we belonged. In Europe a family would live in the same town for many generations, not like today where people move from one city to another. So the students developed a greater sense of belonging to the shul, the yeshiva and the town. I remember I once left Telz for a short period of time. When I returned I went to give a greeting to the Rosh HaYeshiva. He

asked for an explanation of my actions, and I responded that I had been away for a short period of time. He asked me if I left my house without saying goodbye, and if not, why did I leave town without saying goodbye? This was the feeling one had in Telz— you belonged, it was home. The yeshiva affected our lives from birth; the *kedushah* (holiness) was so great that it controlled a person's life. Once someone touched the door handle of the yeshiva he was a Telzer for life. No one was ever pushed out of the yeshiva. In my time it was unheard of that anyone would miss a *yahrtzeit shiur*—this was something that was an important part of your heritage as a Telzer.

Elul was a time of great fear in the town. I remember that as a young *bochur* my friends and I would sigh with such a feeling of relief when Yom Kippur was over. This *yirah* (fear) of the *Yomim Noraim* was a feeling that permeated the entire town like a mist after the rain. You could feel it, it penetrated your bones and became a part of you. Somehow we need to recapture this and convey it to our students today. We grew up breathing this feeling into our *neshamos* the same way one takes in vitamins and minerals with one's food. It was a spiritual diet.

When the Rebbitzin and I were engaged we had a greater sense of trust in Hashem, that He would provide for our needs. Much greater than what I see in America today."

Rebbitzin Gifter related that "A young man once came to speak to Rabbi Gifter, and related to the Rosh HaYeshiva that he

Telz Yeshiva in Lithuania

The yeshiva affected our lives from birth; the kedusha *(holiness) was so great that it controlled a person's life. Once someone touched the door handle of the yeshiva he was a Telzer for life.*

Roshei HaYeshiva, Menahalim, Kollel and the Talmidim of the Telz Yeshiva in 1932 (5692)

The legacy of Telz and the Lithuanian yeshivos is Torah. The pure study of Torah for its own sake.

wants to learn for 2 years, get married, learn for 2 more years, and then raise a family. The Rosh HaYeshiva looked at him and said, 'So! You have everything all planned out. Very good! Therefore, I have nothing to say'."

Rabbi Gifter continued, "We didn't think like that in Europe, that everything had to be planned and secured. We had an idea of what we wanted to do, and trusted that Hashem would lead us and provide for our needs. There was no set plan. The Rebbetzin's father always taught that a person's first step in marriage (or any endeavor) must be straight. The first step of each endeavor must be to fulfill the will of Hashem, and to have *bitachon* (trust) that Hashem will guide, protect and provide for you. When someone proceeds in such a manner they will have success. Let Hashem be the guiding life force, don't plan everything out first and afterwards send the plan to Hashem to put His stamp of approval on it.

Before the Germans occupied Telz, the yeshiva was divided into several groups that sought refuge in different towns and villages. Therefore, when Telz was destroyed, the majority of the students had already fled. The Rosh HaYeshiva, Rabbi Avraham Bloch stayed with those who didn't leave. They were all martyred together.

The legacy of Telz and the Lithuanian yeshivos is Torah. The pure study of Torah for its own sake. To sacrifice and be satisfied with few possessions for the sake of Torah, this was the highest ideal. This is what those generations were like. We lived Torah. It was our life. Telz was unique because it was a town that functioned solely according to the Torah. This is its legacy."

TELZ YESHIVA IN AMERICA, 5756/1996

Rabbi Mordecai Gifter, Shlita— Rosh HaYeshiva

Rabbi Pesach Stein, Shlita— Rosh Yeshiva

Rabbi Aizik Ausband, Shlita— Rosh Yeshiva

Rabbi Chaim Stein, Shlita— Rosh Yeshiva

The majestic Aron Kodesh inside the Telz Beis Hamedrash

The facade of the Telz Beis Medrash building

All photos taken by Zev Saftlas

≈ REFLECTIONS ON SLABODKA:

*The reminiscences of Rabbi Avigdor Miller, Shlita
Rosh HaYeshiva of the Bais Yisroel Torah Center*

"I went to Slabodka 63 years ago, arriving on *Erev Shavous* (1933). The town was very primitive, with many small houses. The yeshiva was a dilapidated building, but when you came inside you were at once enveloped by the prolific spirit of the yeshiva. There were 180 *bochurim* in the Slabodka Yeshiva in my time, and the youngest were 18 or 19 years of age. There were also some *bochurim* 50-years-old, whose lives had been disrupted by World War I, and consequently they were never able to marry. There was a tradition in the yeshiva, when I arrived, that had been transmitted for many years—that the *mashgiach* in the yeshiva fifty years earlier had been at the funeral of Rabbi Yisroel Salanter. This means that the teachings of the *Mussar* Movement were very real to us, because the *mashgiach* had been at the funeral of the movement's founder. Rabbi Yisroel Salanter was the rebbe of the Alter of Kelm, and of the Alter of Slabodka. It is through these two men that much of our Torah in America today had its beginnings, as we shall see.

In the yeshiva everybody was united with the spirit that one must have the greatest respect for the *hanhaleh*. Every *bochur* was a *lamdon*. Each had been a *talmid* in a smaller yeshiva first—in America a comparable yeshiva would have been on a very high level. Rabbi Yechezkel Bernstein, the author of the *sefer, Divrei Yechezkel* was the *menahel* of this yeshiva. By the time the students arrived in Slabodka they were all *lamdonim*, very accomplished learners.

In Slabodka there were three hour and a half *shmussen*, three *mussar* lectures, held each week. Two were given by Rabbi Isaac Sher, the Rosh HaYeshiva, in the yeshiva itself. It was mandatory for all students to attend. The third was given in the home of Rav Avrohom Grodzenski, the *mashgiach*, every *erev Shabbos*. Instead of saying the *Kabbolos Shabbos* prayer, *L'chu Niranena*, we heard a *shmues*. This *shmues* was said in the style of the Alter of Slabodka: he would say three words and then pause,

The yeshiva was a dilapidated building, but when you came inside you were at once enveloped by the spirit of the yeshiva.

Rabbi Yisroel Salanter was the rebbe of the Alter of Kelm, and of the Alter of Slabodka. It is through these two men that much of our Torah in America today had its beginnings.

and then three more words and pause—this is how the entire *shmues* was conducted. If you weren't accustomed to this style it was hard to stay awake. However, once you got used to this type of delivery you had time to think in between. Each word was measured and weighed. It was amazing how careful he was with each word he said, in this manner he conveyed the exact meaning he intended and no extra

"Der Alter of Slabodka"
Rabbi Nosson Tzvi Finkel

words were necessary. Rav Avrohom was the son-in-law of the old *mashgiach* Reb Beryl. Reb Isaac Sher spoke in a more conventional style but, again, each word was weighed and measured. These were remarkable people...royalty. They were dignified, friendly...people of composure, never frivolous. It was remarkable to see people whose entire conduct was one of restraint, a standard for self-control. They were models of *seichal*, of *mussar*...of proper behavior. In Slabodka the word 'bad' was never used, even in Yiddish (*schlecht*). If they had to say it they used the expression 'not good' in its place. One of the principles of Slabodka was that man is a *Tzelem Elokim*, created in the image of Hashem, therefore, they were very careful never to be disparaging of another person, Jew or gentile. Although all human beings are made in Hashem's image, the Jews are on a higher level because they accepted the Torah, and by doing so, became G-d's Chosen People.

The Alter of Slabodka spoke for forty years on the importance of *Tzelem Elokim* alone. I once spoke to an old ex-*talmid* of the yeshiva who said that the Alter spoke

on this topic so much that it was coming out of his ears already. My father-in-law, who was also an old *talmid* of Slabodka, said he never heard of such a thing, that if it was "coming out of your ears" it meant you had not heard enough...that you can never hear enough of such a subject. The fact that all mankind is created with *Tzelem Elokim* is one of the main foundation principles of the Torah. Hashem put His image on the face of every person so that you should look at a man's face and be reminded of Hashem. When a man looks at you it is as if Hashem is looking at you through his eyes. The story is told that when the Alter was leaving Slabodka to go to Eretz Yisrael his *talmidim* accompanied him to the border where the train station was located. As the train was leaving, they walked outside on the platform alongside the train while the Alter was talking

It was remarkable to see people whose entire conduct was one of restraint, a standard for self-control. They were models of seichal, *of* mussar...*of proper behavior.*

Rav Yitzchok Isaac Sher,
Rosh HaYeshiva of Slabodka

Rav Avrohom Grodzenski,
the Mashgiach in Slabodka

*Rav Moshe Mordechai Epstein,
Rosh HaYeshiva of Slabodka in
Lithuania and later in Chevron*

*Rav Issur Zalman Meltzer,
Rosh HaYeshiva in Slabodka
and later in Slutsk*

*When a person is
silent and serious,
but cheerful...
not sad—
this is
Tzelem Elokim.*

*...Mussar was a
different thing.
Then began the
chant, the niggun,
that was used for
the study of
mussar, first slowly
and then more
quickly and louder
until they were
"raising the roof."*

to them. A Lithuanian policeman came and waved the students away from the train. The Alter's last words to them was "we want to make them great, but they won't let us make them great."

What is *Tzelem Elokim*...what are the characteristics on the face of a person that represents *Tzelem Elokim*? Everything! Only *you* can take the most beautiful characteristics and spoil them by a wrong expression. When a person is silent and serious, but cheerful...not sad—this is *Tzelem Elokim*. When one begins contorting his facial features due to his lack of good *midos* (qualities of character) he can ruin even the most beautiful appearance. Before a person speaks, I may have great respect for him, but when one speaks it is possible to lose all respect for him...he dispels the magic. Before a person verbalizes his thoughts, however, by looking at his face alone, we give him credit for greatness. "...A fool when he is silent can be considered a wise man..."*(Mishlei: 17:28).*

Every night we learned *mussar* for half an hour in the yeshiva, and it was learned with great zeal. All day long the *talmidim* engaged in Torah, back and forth, like

on a battlefield. When it came time to learn *mussar* the old *Mashgiach* opened the drawer of the *shulchan* that held the *mussar seforim*, and everyone stopped what he was doing. Not everyone was addicted to *mussar*, but even those who were not had respect...*mussar* was a different thing. Then began the chant, the *niggun*, that was used for the study of *mussar*, first slowly and then more quickly and loudly until they were "raising the roof." People were admonishing themselves for the imperfections of character, repeating a saying over and over again with a *niggun* so that it would penetrate their hearts. I remember how Reb Avrohom Freischeller, an old *bochur* of 40, would say during *mussar seder*, "..if a person speaks *lashon hara* it is as if he denies Hashem..." and he would quote the *pasuk* ...*with our tongue we will conquer, our lips belong to us, who is the master over us (Tehillim: 12:5).* A person who assumes he can say whatever he wishes thinking he is not doing anything wrong, is actually rebelling against Hashem, just like one who worships idols. I heard him say that over and again for a whole half hour, shouting aloud to impress upon himself that he must have control over his tongue. Without that self-control you imply that there is no master over you.

Shabbos, after *shalosh seudos*, we all went to the *Beis Hamedrash* where we would learn *mussar* for an hour in the dark. The *talmidim* went all out, weeping, shouting, stamping their feet, talking to themselves...it was an unforgettable scene that hour. They were working on themselves...working, harder and harder to improve their character. At the end of the hour you heard a low, sad voice start the initial prayer of *Maariv*, *"Vehu Rachum"*—we started the new week with a spiritual elevation of the mind, like going through a fire of purification.

When it was time for a *simcha*—the yeshiva was unequaled. Simchas Torah was a tremendous event in the Yeshiva—we had a list of 85 *niggunim* that we had to sing that day. We worked all day long dancing around and around. First we came for *davening* (*Shachris* and *Musaf*), and then we went home to eat, returned for *Mincha* and then made the *hakafos* until nighttime. There were some Lithuanian police standing around because some of the bums in the town tried to shoot needles at the yeshiva boys through the windows. The town had deteriorated very much, and the behavior of some of the youth was inappropriate. In general, the town was antagonistic to the yeshiva. The yeshiva was packed, and all day long the boys danced around, repeating the same song over and over again. You see the words of the song themselves were *mussar*, so when you repeated it over so many times with such an intensity of happiness it becomes very deeply rooted in your mind. The *simcha* had a tremendous effect on the people.

I remember the day after Simchas Torah. In the morning Reb Isaac (Sher) would speak reminding the *talmidim* that they had worked very hard during the Ten Days of Teshuva, Rosh Hashanah and Yom Kippur—*davening* and learning *mussar* every morning. They had also attended *shmussen* every day during that time—more then usual. The *davening* during those days was truly awesome in its sincerity and true devotion, and then Simchas Torah arrived. 'You have acquired a great amount of *ruchneius*,' he said, 'so you must be careful when you return to your small towns not to become influenced by any *laitzonus*, scoffing or joking.' The Rosh HaYeshiva would emphasize that the *Mesillas Yeshorim* teaches that one joke can topple a tower of *spiritual attainment*: 'Beware of *laitzonus* when you go home. Each precious acquisition that you gain

Yeshiva Knesses Yisroel in Slabodka

here be careful not to lose it, when you go home, because of carelessness. This means that no matter how great a person has become by his efforts he must be aware that it is a very fragile and delicate acquisition. *Spiritual attainment* is hard to acquire but easy to lose. As it says, Torah is compared to a delicate and precious crystal vessel that is difficult to obtain but easy to break.' He warned us that when we went back to our little towns after *Yom Tov* we should be aware of *laitzonus*, because it could break down the tower of perfection built up during the *Yomim Noraim*.

There was a great spirit of idealism in the yeshiva. The boys were mainly very

When it was time for a simcha—*the yeshiva was unequaled. Simchas Torah was a tremendous event in the Yeshiva—we had a list of 85* niggunim *that we had to sing that day.*

poor...very poor indeed. I had friends who ate a piece of bread and a glass of milk with a half a cube of sugar for breakfast. The other half cube they kept for supper. There was almost nothing to eat. At that time we read in the newspaper that a Jew named Warburg gave 20 million dollars for black education in Chicago. I thought, back then, that if he had given a fraction of that to the yeshivas in Eastern Europe he would have gained *Olam Habah* by saving these poor boys from their starvation diets. To the boys, however, the main concern of their lives was gaining spiritual perfection. They labored under the tutelage of great men, and the spirit of their rebbes was what suffused and sustained them. In any yeshiva a person who stays for some length of time is influenced, but the yeshivos in Eastern Europe were old institutions with great traditions, and upon entering one perceived immediately the special atmosphere of generations of learning that permeated the yeshiva—the influence was tremendous.

Rabbi Aharon Kotler, Rosh HaYeshiva of Beis Medrash Gevoah/Lakewood

Rabbi Yitzchok Hutner, Rosh HaYeshiva of Yeshiva Rabbi Chaim Berlin

Rabbi Yaakov Kaminetsky, Rosh HaYeshiva of Yeshiva Torah Vodaath

Rabbi Yaakov Yitzchak Ruderman, Rosh HaYeshiva of Ner Yisrael/Baltimore

The destruction of the Slabodka Yeshiva, of Telz...of all the yeshivos in Europe was an enormous loss to our people. When the Bolsheviks came into power they started to destroy the yeshivos and the spirit of the Jews in western Russia. Many of those Bolsheviks were Jewish. When Hitler came into Russia, he found a culture that had already been destroyed. Most of the yeshivos had been dismantled by the Communists, the talmidim were disbanded and many fled to other areas for refuge. The Jewish mind was destroyed by the Communists, many of whom were Jews. In fact, some of the most active anti-religious

Communists were Jews! So, in one sense, renegade Jews helped to destroy Jewish culture in Russia, and then the Germans came and murdered the Jews.

When we talk about the influence that the yeshiva had on the world in general, the students of Slabodka went out and changed the world. Rabbi Yitzchok Hutner, the Rosh HaYeshiva of Yeshiva Rabbi Chaim Berlin came from Slabodka. Rabbi Yitzchak Ruderman, who founded Ner Yisrael in Baltimore was also from Slabodka, as was Rabbi Yaakov Kaminetzky the Rosh HaYeshiva from Torah Vodaath and Rabbi Aharon Kotler, who founded the Lakewood Yeshiva. All of these great men who helped to rebuild the Torah anew in America after the war came from Slabodka. The Alter

THE SLABODKA YESHIVA AND ITS INFLUENCE

Founded in 1884 by Rabbi Nosson Tzvi Finkel, "Der Alter of Slabodka"

Rabbi Nosson Tzvi Finkel *(Talmid of Rabbi Yisrael Salanter and the Alter of Kelm)*	**Founder and Rosh HaYeshiva in Lithuania and later in Chevron, Eretz Yisrael**
Reb Yitzchok Yaakov Rabinowitz "Reb Itzele Ponevezher"	**Rosh HaYeshiva with the Alter (c.1892-1894)**
Rabbi Isser Zalman Meltzer	**Rosh HaYeshiva with the Alter from 1894-1897** *Sent by the Alter in 1897 to become Rosh HaYeshiva in Slutsk*
Rabbi Moshe Mordechai Epstein	**Rosh HaYeshiva with the Alter**
Rabbi Yitzchok Isaac Sher *(Son-in-law of the Alter)*	**Rosh HaYeshiva**

Influence of "Der Alter" and the Slabodka Derech on European Yeshivos

Telz Yeshiva	Talmidim of the Alter served as "spiritual supervisors"
Slutsk Yeshiva	The Alter sent Rabbi Isser Zalman Meltzer to become the Rosh HaYeshiva, accompanied by 14 talmidim
Mirrer Yeshiva	The Alter sent his son, Rabbi Eliezer Yehuda Finkel along with 10 other talmidim— Rabbi Finkel eventually became the Rosh HaYeshiva *(see section on Mir, page 18)*
Stuchin/Anaf Knesses Yisrael	Led by Rabbi Yehuda Leib Chasman, a talmid of the Alter
Kobrin Yeshiva	Led by Rabbi Pesach Pruskin, a talmid of the Alter
Kletzk Yeshiva	Founded by Rabbi Aharon Kotler, a talmid of the Alter

Influence of "Der Alter" and the Slabodka Derech on American Yeshivos

Beis Medrash Gevoah/Lakewood	Rabbi Aharon Kotler,[1] Founder and Rosh HaYeshiva
Yeshiva Rabbi Chaim Berlin	Rabbi Yitzchok Hutner,[1] Rosh HaYeshiva
Yeshiva Torah Vodaath	Rabbi Yaakov Kaminetsky,[1] Rosh HaYeshiva
Yeshiva Ner Yisrael/Baltimore	Rabbi Yaakov Yitzchak Ruderman,[1] Founder and Rosh HaYeshiva
Yeshiva Chofetz Chaim	Rabbi Dovid Leibowitz,[1] Founder and Rosh HaYeshiva
Beis Yisroel Torah Center	Rabbi Avigdor Miller,[2] Rosh HaYeshiva and Rov

1. A Talmid of the Alter of Slabodka
2. A Talmid of Rabbi Yitzchok Isaac Sher

The Alter of Slabodka was a mechanech (teacher) par excellence. He could perceive hidden abilities in a person and develop them to the utmost.

of Slabodka was a *mechanech* (teacher) par excellence. He could perceive hidden abilities in a person and develop them to the utmost. He worked hard to perfect his students in *all* of their actions. One of the boys used to walk with his head somewhat bent over, so the Alter ordered him to wear pince-nez glasses that would fall off if he didn't keep his head up. The boys learned to carry themselves with a dignified and solemn demeanor, not like a slouch. A *talmid* should look like an important person..appearance was very important. The Kelm Talmud Torah was even more strict in this manner. The Kelmer boys were trained to look very dignified. In those days college students dressed in a very refined manner, not like a college student today, and Kelmer *talmidim* were trained to look even more dignified then college students. In Slabodka every *talmid* carried a cane, like a gentleman, later they stopped, but at one time they all carried a cane.

I was 24-years-old when I went to Slabodka. Rabbi Isaac Sher came to America to raise money for the yeshiva. He didn't succeed. We used to visit him

Panorama of Kovna on the Niemen River. Slabodka is a suburb of Kovna.

every week in the apartment where he was staying on Henry Street on the East Side (New York) and he gave us a *shmues*. We fell in love with his *shmussen*, and we decided that we wanted to go to Slabodka. The chief organizer of this endeavor was Rabbi Yehuda Davis, an old friend of mine, who has a yeshiva in upstate New York in Mountaindale. He was the most influential and he got a group of us together to go to Slabodka. The joke was that Reb Isaac didn't come home from America with money, he brought *talmidim* instead.

Reb Isaac himself was a very great intellect. Everything he said in Torah you could understand, it was well explained and made great sense. That is why we were so motivated to listen to him. He explained things with complete clarity. I remember he was once speaking in Slabodka about a passage in *Mesillas Yeshorim* where it asks, "...what is the duty of a person in this world?—to gain entrance into the happiness of the World to Come." He explained that in the *sefer* is written that man was created only to have pleasure from Hashem, but Reb Isaac would stop after the word 'pleasure', and explain that Hashem wanted to bestow pleasure on mankind, that is why He made the world a happy place. Hashem wants you to enjoy the pleasure of this world in such a way that it will bring you to the greater happiness in the World to Come. Therefore, you have to utilize all the opportunities for happiness in this world in order to sing to Hashem in this world, and love Him and think about Him, so that you will come to the great happiness that will bring you to the next world...the place of real happiness. All the happiness of this world is merely a preparation for the World to Come. This is similar to what we say in the first *posuk* of *Ashrei*, *"Ashrei yoshvei veisacha, od..."* It's the singing to Hashem in this world that prepares you

Typical street scene in Kovna, c.1930

for singing to Hashem in the World to Come. We're just rehearsing now. If you enjoy the springtime, if you enjoy your youth, your good health, etc., whatever it is that you are able to enjoy, and there is plenty to enjoy, you should appreciate these things and thank Hashem for everything. After a while you'll be so well rehearsed in singing to Hashem that after 120 years you'll be completely prepared to sing to Hashem in the World to Come. In Slabodka they never spoke about *Gehinnom*, only about the reward in the next world. When Reb Isaac was in America he spoke about *Gehinnom*. He was once invited to a banquet and spoke about *Gehinnom* because when people are enjoying this world frivolously, it's important to talk about *Gehinnom*. However, to the poor boys in Slabodka he only spoke about the happiness and greatness of perfection and the great reward that awaits them. He knew how to reach his students, oh yes, he knew very well. He was always very polite and diplomatic to the boys, very polite.

By the time Rosh Hashanah arrived we already were filled to overflowing with *Yiras Shomayim*—all of *Elul* we heard extra *shmussen*, more then any other time in the year. We also learned extra *mussar*, besides the half hour every night, we learned another 15 minutes during the daytime too. All of the *shmussen* were concerned with the *Yom HaDin*, the Day of Judgment. We were well prepared. When the first night of Rosh Hashanah finally arrived the *shliach tzibur* said *Borchu* and everyone responded with the next

In Slabodka they never spoke about Gehinnom, only about the reward in the next world.

...In Slabodka we always took a long time to daven, to consider the depth and meaning of what we were saying.

In the olden days, the ordinary worker put in more effort into his daily davening *than we do into our Yom Kippur* tefillos.

pasuk as required and then we settled down to say the first blessing. *"Hashem Elokainu...Hashem is our G-d, He belongs to us..."* Every word was saturated with all the thoughts that we had gathered during the whole year from the *mussar* we learned. The *bochurim* were standing on their feet and raising the roof with their shouts. Each blessing took a long time. Finally, the students came to the end of the blessing and there was a deep silence. The *shliach tzibur* said the end of the blessing aloud and there was a thunderous *Amen,* and then silence. Then the next blessing began, and each word was said with such deep emotion, slowly with a haunting *niggun...Torah and mitzvos, aye, yie, yie....* It took a long time to say this blessing, a long time. We didn't use any *chazonus* in Slabodka, we just said the words straight, we only needed the meaning of the words alone...no singing. *"Shema Yisrael"* took a long time, and the *Shemoneh Esrei* took an exceedingly long time, with the *talmidim* thinking about each word...each word was taken into their hearts. The same was true on any of the fast days as well. The prayers had to be infused with thought, so in Slabodka we always took a long time to *daven,* to consider the depth and meaning of what we were saying. As it is stated, any prayer that does not have proper *kavonah,* thoughtful intent, is not considered prayer.

I remember that after Yom Kippur we went back to where we were staying to get something to eat after the fast. I was sitting with the others, and we just sat there, all together, no one said a word, not a word. That's how much we remained under the awe of Yom Kippur. Slabodka, like other

Yeshiva Beis Yitzchok in Slabodka

places of *mussar,* was similar to a foundry where precious metal was melted down, refined and then re-formed again. Only in Slabodka more emphasis was put on thoughts than on deeds. Once, before my time, Reb Yitzchok Peterberger (Reb Yitzchok Blauser, one of Rabbi Yisroel Salanter's main *talmidim*) was present in the yeshiva at *Neilah.* When the *davening* was over he said a few words. He told the *talmidim* that the way they *davened* that day, on Yom Kippur, was the way people would *daven* on a regular Monday and Thursday when the long *Tachanun* prayer is said in the Shoemakers' Shul in Kovno.

In the olden days, the ordinary worker put more effort into his daily *davening* than we do into our Yom Kippur *tefillos.* It seems hard to believe. The assistant secretary of the Slabodka Yeshiva told me that had I been in the yeshiva even ten years earlier I would have been surprised with what I would have seen. The world had deteriorated since then. There was a fire burning in the hearts of the Jewish people at one time. It's a fact...it's a fact. An ordinary Jew had such an idealism, he, his wife and sons and daughters...a fire burned in every Jewish home and heart. We have no idea what the old Jewish attitude was. Later, the Enlightenment started destroying the spirit of the Jewish people. And the newspapers...the newspapers ruined the Jewish people in Europe. There were so many anti-religious papers put out by the adherents to the different groups: the Socialists, the Bundists, the Communists, etc. The effect was horrible. Before that, however, we were a nation that typified the statement, *Aish dos lamo*, "A fiery Torah for them" *(Devarim 33:2).*

I remember I once read a history book by Will Durant who wrote that the Jews are in love with their religion. One historian describing Cracow in the time of the Rama, Rabbi Moshe Isserles (1530-1572), stated that the Torah flowed out of the synagogues and into the streets...that children babbled in Torah in the streets. There was so much Torah in the world that the streets were full of Torah. Lately there has been a bit of an awakening among the Jewish people, *Boruch Hashem*, there is a new idealism in *yiddishkeit.* I am amazed at what has taken place in America in the last 60 years. It was unexpected. I remember 60 years ago you couldn't find an Orthodox girl in America...it was very difficult. There was only one yeshiva before the '20's, Yeshiva University, the only one. Everyone thought there was no future for Judaism in America, and today, *Boruch Hashem...* Jews today are careful with the most minute aspect of *mitzvos* that weren't even thought about in America 50 or 60 years ago...today there is a revolution in *yiddishkeit.* There is great hope for American Jewry, the Orthodox population may rebuild what they once had, and it is important to know what they once had—great treasures. When the Nazis came and marched the yeshiva boys to the 9th Fort in Kovno with Reb Elchonon Wasserman, where they shot them to death, this furthered their guilt beyond measure. The Germans will never be forgiven for all that they did to us. Every one of those *talmidim* was a precious acquisition that belonged to the Jewish people, and when the Germans came and killed them their guilt is such that it will last forever, it will never be atoned.

Those who escaped and came to America to rebuild Torah, as we mentioned,

Reb Aharon in Lakewood, Rabbi Ruderman in Baltimore, Rabbi Hutner in Chaim Berlin...they were rescued in order to build again for the future. We hope that the day will come when all of those great sanctuaries will again be rebuilt and the Jewish people will recognize the greatness for which they were created.

The Jewish youth of today should be aware of the principle expressed in the *pasuk,* "I Hashem have not changed, you the Jewish nation will never come to an end"*(Malachi 3:1).* This means that just as Hashem will never change, the Jewish nation will remain a holy people forever.

Reb Elchonon Wasserman at the Third Knessiah Gedolah in Marienbad, 1937

There may be ups and downs, but the Jews will reassert themselves at some point. There is no question, *Am Israel*, the Jewish people, are a holy nation. That is the Jewish spirit, and even though it is sometimes buried under the foolishness of the country where they live or

Lately there has been a bit of an awakening among the Jewish people, Boruch Hashem, there is a new idealism in yiddishkeit. I am amazed at what has taken place in America in the last 60 years.

The awareness that we belong to the Eternal Nation is enough to support the confidence and idealism of the Jewish people... the awareness that we are forever.

the times in which they live, it will proclaim itself again. That is the principle. *Am Israel* is an Eternal Nation, that is why we are called the *Am Olam*, a nation that is forever. Therefore, we have to know that just as Hashem is eternal, we also are eternal because He took us to Him as it says, *"Shema Yisrael, Hashem Elokainu"—He is ours.* He is the One Who created everything. Hashem maintains the existence of everything, not like the carpenter who created this bench and is no longer here, no. Hashem keeps the universe in exist-

ence every second, He is the only one and He is ours...ours. Ours means two things, He is for us and we are for Him. This is the main principle of the *Shema*, He is for us and we are for Him. Therefore, Hashem is Eternal and we will be eternal too. This is what we say in *Boruch Sh'omar*, "Blessed is the One who gives a good reward to those who fear Him"*(from the introductory prayer in the Morning service).* Although Hashem has pity on all creatures, He gives His good reward only to those who fear Him. How long will it last? Forever. Just as He is eternal, so will the reward last forever, as we say..."*Boruch chai lo'aad v'kayim l'netzach"*, Blessed is the One who lives forever and endures throughout eternity. The awareness that we belong to the Eternal Nation is enough to support the confidence and idealism of the Jewish people...the awareness that we are forever."

Rabbi Avigdor Miller delivering a mussar shmues in his shul— Bais Yisroel Torah Center

REMEMBERING KELM AND TELZ:

The reminiscences of the founder and dean of the Hebrew Academy of Cleveland, Rabbi Nochum Zev Dessler, Shlita

The story is told in *Mussar* circles that at a convention of German University deans to discuss curriculum, a professor rose and said, 'There is one area of knowledge that is studied in only one institution in the world, in a small Russian town named Kelm. That subject is the correcting of man's character traits.'[17]

"Kelm was a place where you were able to see the greatness within a person, and the closer you were to people who lived there, the greater they appeared. This is the opposite of our impression of famous people today, where closer inspection reveals their imperfections. I once asked my father why my *zaidy* wouldn't do anything without first going to the Chofetz Chaim. He told me that as you get close to people you usually tend to see more negative things about them, but not so with the Chofetz Chaim, who became greater and more impressive with each meeting.

To a certain extent that's what it was like in Kelm. You saw people who were from a different world, a different time, people who have no connection to the world we live in today. In Kelm people were concerned about everyone else except themselves, and you saw it everywhere: in the home, in business and in the *Beis Hamedrash*. The Lomza *Mashgiach* writes that once when he arrived in Kelm, people came over to greet him, and then more people came forward, followed by still others. He thought it was a special welcoming committee—but that was Kelm—when someone came, everyone greeted him and inquired about his welfare, as an expression of their concern.

The whole *Talmud Torah*[18] in Kelm was

> "Kelm was a place where you were able to see the greatness within a person, and the closer you were to people who lived there, the greater they appeared."

---

17. Rabbi Chaim Ephraim Zaitchik, **Sparks of Mussar** (Feldheim Publishers, New York, 1985) page 78.
18. Unlike our present day conception of a Talmud Torah, Reb Simcha Zissel's Talmud Torah was a yeshiva for grown men where the perfection of character in one's relationship with The Creator and one's fellow Jew was emphasized. Reb Simcha Zissel produced many talmidim of great stature in Torah and Fear of Heaven, whose teachings have had a profound effect on Klal Yisrael until this day.

only three times the size of this dining room. It was about 45 feet by 60 feet in total size, and yet such a relatively small space contained so much spiritual greatness that it is impossible to describe. How do you explain the manner in which people worked on themselves to uproot every bad character trait, and were relentlessly criticized for bad *midos* by their rebbe and friends, or the self-criticism directed at one's own lack of progress and change?

The author of **Sparks of Mussar** relates that my grandfather, Reb Nochum Zev, came home to visit his father, Reb Simcha Zissel, for Yom Tov. Reb Simcha Zissel noticed that his son ate with slightly hurried motions, a result of the fact that he had often gone hungry while away in yeshiva. Reb Simcha Zissel was displeased. "If you like," he said, "I will give you such a speech about the lowliness of life that you won't be able to look at food for two weeks."[19]

This is how it was there—to eat hurriedly was a character flaw that needed correction. One had to strive to be in control of his emotions and desires at all times, and this is what the men of my great-grandfather's *Talmud Torah* strove to accomplish. At its height the *Talmud Torah* had around 30 to 35 men learning full time. The yeshiva continued in operation until 1941.

The men who learned in the *Talmud Torah* mainly came there after they were married. They settled in Kelm and a few

19. Rabbi Chaim Ephraim Zaitchik, page 78.

Reb Simcha Zissel Ziv's Talmud Torah in Kelm

of them conducted some sort of business. During the lunch break (*bein ha'sedorim*) they would take over the business and relieve their wives, who would then go home to cook.

The *mashgichim* of most of the yeshivos in Poland and Lithuania came from the Kelm *Beis Hamedrash*: in Mir you had Reb Yeruchem Levovitz; in Slobodka you had the Alter, Reb Nosson Zvi Finkel; in Lomza you had Reb Moshe Rosenstein; and in Kletzk you had Reb Yosef Leib Nenedik and Reb Yechezkel Levenstein, who became the Mirrer *Mashgiach* and eventually *Mashgiach* of Ponevezh in Bnei Brak.

Kelm was a small town, a couple of city blocks altogether, with three or four hundred Jewish families. When I was nine-years-old I was already learning in the *Yeshiva K'tana* in Kelm, and I still have my first *Gemora* notes from that *shiur*. The

Rabbi Eliyahu Eliezer Dessler

Beis Midrash of the yeshiva had a night *seder* where we learned by candlelight because there was no electricity. I still have my *Gemora* from that time, with the wax from the candles that dripped over the pages. There were about 150 *talmidim* in the yeshiva. Rabbi Eliyahu Lopian was the founder of the yeshiva and his brother-in-law, Rabbi Elya Kremerman, was the Rosh HaYeshiva.

My father was born in Vilna. My grandfather, Reb Reuven Dov Dessler, married one of the granddaughters of Rabbi Yisroel Salanter, as did Rabbi Chaim Ozer Grodzenski. My mother's father was Reb Nochum Zev Ziv, the son of the Alter of Kelm, Reb Simcha Zissel Braude-Ziv. Reb Simcha Zissel's father was a *dayan* in Kelm.

Altogether the Braude-Ziv family was in Kelm for 12 or 13 generations. This is something you don't have any more, that one family remains for generation after generation in one place, as we lived in Eastern Europe.

Kelm was a Jewish town, the gentiles lived in the surrounding villages. In Telz it was the same, though it was a much bigger town and the houses were somewhat larger.

My father came to Kelm at Bar Mitzvah age, learned there for 18 years, and then married Reb Nochum Zev's daughter. His Rosh HaYeshiva was Reb Hirsch Braude, Reb Simcha Zissel's son-in-law.

My childhood in Kelm was very sheltered. We grew up in an atmosphere of pure Torah with no distractions. We lived surrounded by Jews and that's all we saw. Even the games we played had Torah themes in them. There was an underground brook outside of Kelm where we would play. We used to run to the brook and, drop down and put our ears to the ground to see if we could hear the sound of the running water. When we finally were close enough to hear the water, we would call out that we heard *Korach* crying. **Everything** revolved around Torah. We had no games and toys like today, but we had balls to play with—all of our games were Torah-related. At night we learned or talked together as a family. The sound of learning resounded in the night air.

In the early 1900s the men walked on one side of the street, and the women walked on the other. By the time I reached Kelm, however, husbands and wives were already walking together.

The mashgichim *of most of the yeshivos in Poland and Lithuania came from the Kelm Beis Hamedrash...*

***Everything** revolved around Torah. We had no games and toys like today, but we had balls to play with—all of our games were Torah-related.*

Typical street in Kelm

When I was young there were no sidewalks in Kelm, only two wood planks wide enough for two people to walk together, side by side. I remember I was once walking with my grandmother (my mother's mother) on the street of the *Talmud Torah*. As we made our way down the sidewalk, my grandmother said that we should cross to the other side. If the *Talmud Torah* was on this side, I inquired, why did we have to cross to the other side? Her answer was a classic example of how people thought in those days. She said that the people from the *Talmud Torah* have very great *derech eretz* (exceptional manners) for other people, and if we are walking on the same side of the street, they are going to walk off the planks and into the dirt and mud to make room for us. If we do this we will be inconveniencing *Bnei Torah*. She told me always to remember not to inconvenience someone who learns Torah. Therefore, we crossed the street and walked on the other side. This is how we grew up, learning the importance of Torah and *midos*. I was only five or six-years-old at the time, but the impression remains. That's what life was like then in Eastern Europe, it was a very natural Torah life.

People lived in such a way that their entire behavior was directed toward the welfare of someone else, that they shouldn't inconvenience another.

People lived in such a way that their entire behavior was directed toward the welfare of someone else, that they shouldn't inconvenience another. They lived to help others, and when you grow up in such an environment, it becomes part of you.

Someone once asked me to tell them about my father. I told him that you can see his greatness from his *seforim*, but I can only tell you that I never saw him angry, and I rarely saw him without his jacket. Then the most illustrious people found their greatest enjoyment in learning a single chapter in *Chaye Adam* with a wagon driver or a water carrier. The great, the simple, they all went to shul, and they all learned. Some learned all day, some in the morning and some after work in the evening, but they all learned. I remember when I was older and learning in Telz that when I went into the store to buy something the grocer always had a *Mishnah Brurah* open, and between customers he would learn. If the owner of a store didn't have to be there, if his wife or children could be in the store, he would be learning in the yeshiva. This is how the simple Jew lived his life, it was a very spiritually oriented life then.

Many stories have circulated about the exemplary business lives of the men in Kelm. See if this sounds like a business deal you would hear about in America! I remember one man bringing another to a *Din Torah*, because he had in mind to take **less** money for the article he was selling, while the other person complained that he had in mind to pay **more** money and each would declare that he couldn't go back on his word. This was natural, it wasn't something unusual. It was only after I grew up that I realized that this is not how the majority of people live, that they want to pay less and/or charge more. This is the kind of life we lived.

Reb Hirsch Braude, Reb Simcha Zissel's son-in-law, had a shoe store. He went to Warsaw once or twice a year to buy stock for his inventory. The shoes were marked with pre-WWI prices, from before Reb Hirsch passed away in 1913. I worked in the store for three weeks in the thirties. It was my job to figure out how much Reb Hirsch had paid for the shoes prior to 1913, and then add 10% to the price, even though the value now was much greater. Nechama Leiba (Reb Hirsch's wife and the Alter's daughter) couldn't add more to the price because Reb Hirsch had instructed her not to, before he died. In addition, I had to keep a tally of how much money was made after each sale, because Nechama Leiba would frequently call out and ask me how much we had made in sales. When we reached a certain amount she excused herself to the customers and closed the store. I tried to argue with her that she had waited all week for *marktog* (market day) to do business, but she wouldn't listen. After she made a certain amount, she closed the store and told the customers that there were other stores, and they had to make a living as well.

You must understand that what the Germans did was destroy an entire way of life, because the atmosphere we grew up in cannot be duplicated. We can replicate the learning and the knowledge, but we cannot duplicate the environment and the perfection of character and community life it produced. It was an environment where people were *mistapake b'muat* (satisfied with little), they felt that the little

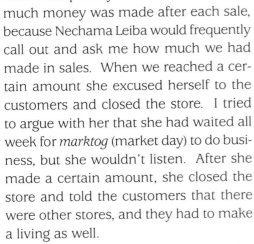

*Reb Hirsch Braude,
son-in-law of Reb Simcha Zissel,
the Alter of Kelm*

they had was enough for their needs and they didn't look for more. They lived according to the Torah and their perspective of life was a Torah perspective. It's not that I am trying to tell an American yeshiva student that there were perfect people fifty years ago, because there is no such thing as perfect people. What I'm trying to show you is that they demanded so much from themselves, because they knew they weren't perfect, but to us they appear perfect. We can't be compared to them, it's not just that we are a generation apart, we are practically living a different existence. I marveled at the exactness with which a Pesach Seder was held in Kelm. The manner in which *talmidim* dressed would tell you which yeshiva they were from, especially Slabodka. In Kelm everyone wore a jacket and tie. In Telz the Rov's children always addressed their parents in the third person. They didn't say *you* to their father or mother. All these practices were the norm of that generation.

A relative who spoke at my Bar Mitzvah in Kelm related that he was last there for my *bris,* and at that time he forgot to take his cane with him. When he returned for the Bar Mitzvah he went directly to the spot where he left it, and there it was! That in itself was not remarkable and it didn't impress him. People didn't touch the possessions of others. What impressed him was that, over the years, it had been taken from its place, cleaned, and then returned exactly as he left it.

All of this was only sixty years ago, but the very fact that you tell stories like

What I'm trying to show you is that they demanded so much from themselves, because they knew they weren't perfect, but to us they appear perfect.

...what the Germans did was destroy an entire way of life, because the atmosphere we grew up in cannot be duplicated.

this to Jewish boys and girls today and they don't really appreciate this consciousness of their grandparents and great-grandparents shows just how far removed we have become. It is very hard to teach these things to children in America because "the street" has such a horrible influence on them. Radio, television, sports games, all of this takes up the minds of the students, the *gaas iz nischt gut* (the street is a bad influence).

I remember that I had a *chavrusah* (learning partner) before my Bar Mitzvah. It was *Elul* and we aspired to be like our mentors, so we decided not to talk during *seder*. If we had to say something we would write it, but we wouldn't talk. This is what we aspired to. We had aspirations of becoming great, not just in Torah, but also in *midos*, and we tried to accomplish as much as we could. This had nothing to do with conceit or pride. This is what was expected of us and we wanted to live up to the expectation.

My wife was born in Berlin, but it wasn't until she came to Poland on vacation that she saw poor Jews. In Berlin they wouldn't allow anyone to go collecting charity in the street, so the first poor Jews she encountered were in Poland. They were Orthodox, but not educated, and for her it was a culture shock. Poland was the area of greatest Jewish poverty because there were so many Jews living there. Work was hard to find, so people had to live wherever they could find a job. I remember her telling me that at first she was aghast when someone came to the door for *tzedakah* and all he received was a sugar cube or a penny. However, when she saw sixty or seventy people coming to the door in the course of a week she understood. The poverty was very great in Poland. This took place in Tarnow, near Cracow. I re-

call when we first came to Cleveland we had difficulty in giving *matanos l'evyonim*, gifts to the poor, on Purim because there were no Jewish poor in Cleveland.

Yesterday was my grandfather's *yartzeit*. He was a wealthy businessman. I remember that he had two suitcases full of Russian rubles in his attic and as a child I would play with the money. When I came to yeshiva before my Bar Mitzvah he took me up to the attic and told me the story behind the suitcases. The Germans were losing WWI and they had a lot of money that they converted into British pounds or Russian rubles because they thought the ruble would remain a stable currency. Grandfather also converted his German money into rubles, which soon became worthless. He told me that he kept the rubles to teach himself the lesson that money is worthless, and he urged me to take some with me so that I should always remember ...*rabos machshavos b'lev ish...*, that "there are many thoughts in the heart of man (but only the Counsel of Hashem will endure)." Grandfather was a very spiritual person, he never put his finger into his pocket unless he first had a reason for doing so. People then were governed by their thought processes and not their desires. They trained themselves to be like this, it wasn't natural.

Once, in Eretz Yisrael, Rabbi Eliyahu Lopian was waiting for a bus. Eventually, many of those waiting became impatient and began looking down the road to see if the bus was coming. Rabbi Lopian looked as well, but immediately caught himself and stopped. He reflected that in Kelm he would have received a strong rebuke for such impatience.

During WWI my grandfather lived in Russia. His brother-in-law, Reb Chaim Ozer (Grodzenski), had fled from Vilna[20] and

20. Finkelman, page 72.

KELM: THE FINAL DAYS

The following account of the martyrdom of the members of the Kelm Talmud Torah was recorded by the sole survivor of that group, who escaped on the march to the death pits. Rabbi Dessler elaborates upon his testimony:

Rabbi Daniel Movshovitz

In the days before the war the *Talmud Torah* was headed by two of my uncles, Reb Daniel Movshovitz and his brother-in-law Reb Gershon Miadnik; they had married daughters of Reb Nochum Zev, as had my father. On June 21, 1941, the Germans entered Kelm. The Shabbos before, Reb Daniel had a dream that there would be a tremendous destruction of *Klal Yisrael,* that the Jews of Kelm would not escape and should accept upon themselves this Heavenly Judgment. Reb Daniel called together the men of the *Talmud Torah* and told them about his dream. Not one of the families left Kelm, or even tried to flee, because Reb Daniel's words were always words of truth. His brother-in-law, Reb Gershon, who was away from Kelm at the time, hurried back so that he should be together with the rest of the *Talmud Torah.*

Before the Jews of Kelm were taken to the pits where they were to be shot, Reb Daniel spoke to them calmly, that they should accept Hashem's Judgment and ready themselves to Sanctify His Great Name. The men went to the pits singing:

...and purify our hearts to serve You in truth   וטהר לבנו לעבדך באמת

fortunate are we, how good is our portion...   אשרינו מה טוב חלקינו

When they arrived at the pits, Reb Daniel asked the German in charge if he could speak to his congregation. He was told that he could, but to keep it short. Again Reb Daniel spoke as he had in the yeshiva—to accept Hashem's judgment with love and not to be fearful. While he was speaking the German interrupted and yelled that he was speaking for too long a time. Reb Daniel then turned back to the families and said, "The time that I have spoken about is upon us, it is a time of *Kiddush Hashem.* Do not be fearful or panic." Reb Daniel spoke these words slowly and calmly. He then turned to the German and said with total control of the situation, "I have finished, now you may begin." With those words the *Talmud Torah* of Kelm and its Jewish community ascended from this world.

was staying with him at the time this story took place. My grandfather was very wealthy and had a beautifully furnished apartment. The Alter of Novardok, Rabbi Yosef Yozel Hurowitz, came to see him and was taken aback at the riches he saw. The system of *mussar* study in Novardok stressed the exact opposite, that one should live very simply, less being best. Since it was Purim, the Alter took my grandfather by the hands and began to dance with him, leading him on top of one of the expensive sofas where they continued their dance. He understood what The Alter was trying to convey and he did not show any displeasure.

Rabbi Diskind, the Rov of Pardes Chana in Eretz Yisrael who eulogized my mother, related that her parents had Jewish maids who served in the house. When she was a girl the children would wash the floors and do all of the heavy cleaning, while the maids did only light work. Her father, Reb Nochum Zev, would remark then that *"a yiddishe tochtor vet tun shvere arbit far uns?"* (Should a Jewish daughter do difficult work for us?).

These were different people, and what bothers me is that more of Kelm hasn't stayed with me. It's hard to maintain that consciousness of life when you are not constantly being supported by the environment. One of the reasons we were able to develop the Torah life we did in the towns and villages of Eastern Europe

Rabbi Eliyohu Meir Bloch

Rabbi Chaim Mordechai Katz

is because we were apart, separated from the influence of the general non-Jewish community, and for many towns and villages this was true for centuries. We didn't mingle with them— there was no commonality of culture. We also weren't influenced by the more modern spirit that was developing in the bigger cities. In America you have no such protection. The Jew is vulnerable to all of the influences of the community around him, unless he makes tremendous effort to limit it as much as possible. Separate Orthodox schools for boys and girls didn't start until after WWI, because before that a child was educated at home. We lived in a closed and protected society.

Rav Eliyohu Meir Bloch and Rabbi Chaim Mordechai Katz left Telz[21] for America right before the beginning of WWII to raise funds for the yeshiva. They had no idea that Telz would be destroyed and they would never see their families again. To travel then, across Russia and Siberia to Japan, in order to go to America was fraught with danger at each step. Yet listen to what kind of *anshei emes* (men of truth) they were. When the American Consulate official in Japan asked Reb Elya Meir if he thought he would be able to return to Lithuania, he responded that he certainly hoped so, but had his doubts. After hearing this, the official canceled the Rabbis' visas on the spot, and they remained in Japan for six months until

One of the reasons we were able to develop the Torah life we did in the towns and villages of Eastern Europe is because we were locked-up, separated from the influence of the general community.

21. See chapter on Telz, page 22.

Rabbi Gifter could secure new visas for them from America. You see, they had visitors' visas, and if you didn't think you would return to your place of origin, you were not considered a visitor. Even though they were traveling for the yeshiva in such a time of need, and were in danger the entire time, still they felt compelled to tell the whole truth. This is what these generations were like.

The Hebrew Academy of Cleveland, founded by Rabbi Nochum Zev Dessler

When I came to Telz I was given a room over a bakery with three other *bochurim*. It smelled wonderful. I asked one of them where I would sleep, and he told me not to worry. Each room in the apartment was already crowded, but he still told me not to worry. That night, after learning, when I came back to the apartment, some of the *bochurim* brought chairs into the room, took one of the doors off its hinges and put the door across the chairs. Then they took a little straw mat out of the storage room, put it on top of the door with a sheet, and for a year and a half that was my bed. I was coming from London where I had my own room with a bathroom close by, but I came to learn, and this is how we lived. You see the *Ahavas Torah* (love for Torah) that my parents had. I was their only son, but they sent me away before Bar Mitzvah so that I should be privileged to benefit from learning in such an environment of *mesiras nefesh* (personal sacrifice) for Torah. There were no phones to call home then, and we didn't send telegrams. I remained in Telz for five years.

When I left Lithuania before the war it was a very, very bitter time for the European *talmidim*. They were trying desperately to get out, but they couldn't. That was when the Mir was saved, but this you will learn more about in the interview with Rebbetzin Ginsburg."

When I left Lithuania before the war it was a very, very bitter time for the European talmidim. They were trying desperately to get out, but they couldn't.

🌿 REMEMBERING THE MIR

*The reminiscences of Rebbetzin Zlota Ginsburg
daughter of Rabbi Yechezkel Levenstein, ZT"L, Mirrer Mashgiach*

> The interview on Mir is considerably longer since Mir was the only Yeshiva to be transplanted intact, and not rebuilt, after World War II. Additionally, Rebbetzin Ginsburg has supplied us with a vivid and extensive portrait of pre-WWII Jewish life in Eastern Europe.
>
> We have focused on Rabbi Levenstein, since he was the one responsible for guiding the Mir Yeshiva from Poland, through Kobe, Japan and Shanghai, China and finally to safety in America.

Kelm: *The Town*

"I was born in Kelm, Lithuania, eight months before the beginning of World War I, on the 7th of Adar in 1914. My father learned in the Kelm Talmud Torah, but it was not like a Talmud Torah in America where children come to learn. In Kelm, the *Talmud Torah* was started by Rabbi Simcha Zissel Ziv, one of the foremost *talmidim* of Rabbi Yisroel Salanter, the father of the *Mussar* Movement (the study of ethical and moral refinement of one's character and actions). The yeshiva continued under Reb Simcha Zissel's son, Rabbi Nochum Zev Ziv, and his son-in-law, Rabbi Hirsch Braude, who was my father's main rebbe. These were giants in a generation of giants, and it was under their influence that I grew up.

People used to call us *mussarnickers*, because the yeshiva was famous for the study of *Mussar*. It is said that the Chazon Ish (Rabbi Avraham Yeshaya Karelitz) once remarked to a young yeshiva student, while urging him to attend my father's lectures, that "Reb Yechezekel has a pure heart. What comes out of such a heart will certainly penetrate other hearts. His faith in the Almighty is unfaltering." The Chazon Ish then extended his hand and withdrew it with a sharp jerk, and added, "His faith is ingrained like the reflex of removing one's

In Kelm, the Talmud Torah was started by Rabbi Simcha Zissel Ziv, one of the foremost talmidim of Rabbi Yisroel Salanter, the father of the Mussar Movement.

Rebbetzin Zlota Ginsburg Collection

— **"Reb Chatzkel"** —
*Rabbi Yechezkel Levenstein,
the Mirrer Mashgiach, who led the Mirrer
Yeshiva from Poland to Kobe, Japan, then to
Shanghai, China and finally to
the shores of America*

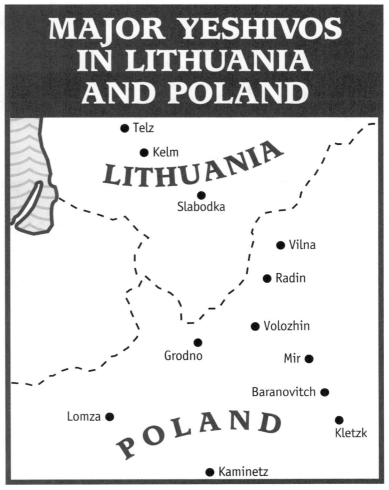

*Location of the Major Yeshivos before World War II.
The towns within the Polish boundaries
are today in Russian territory.*

hand from a flame."[22] This is what my father learned in the *Talmud Torah,* and this is what he taught my sister and me at home.

Kelm consisted of about 500 Jewish families. It was a small town. The Lithuanians lived outside of the town in the surrounding countryside, *m'chutz lamacheneh.* Most of the Jews made their living in business, they had stores...they were *sochrim.* The busiest business day was *marktug,* market day. The gentiles would come into town to buy what they needed, bringing what they had to sell with them: mules, horses, chickens, eggs, vegetables, *tevuah...*whatever they grew and raised on their farms. The rest of the week the Jews would be *m'farnes zeh m'zeh*, they would earn a living from one another. There were dry goods stores and a bakery—many different kinds of businesses. People would buy from the bakery during the week, but for Shabbos everyone would bake their own *challah* and cake.

The gentiles also came in during the week, but Thursday was the main market day. As a child, I found it so interesting. I remember the farmers bringing their *leibidicka ofos* (live chickens), eggs, *behaimos (livestock),* grain and produce. The stores didn't carry eggs in those days, you had to buy them from the farmers. In fact, there was nothing ready-made then, you bought the material or ingredients and

22. Rabbi Elchonon Hertzman, **The Mashgiach** (Jerusalem, 1981) pages 12-13.

Typical market day in a Polish town

Pumping water from a well

made it yourself. We went to the market to buy the chicken, took it to the *shochet,* brought it home, plucked the feathers, salted it and cooked it. My father didn't eat from the *shechitah* if the *shochet* slaughtered three chickens, one after another, without checking the *chalif* (knife). He had my mother tell the *shochet* to check that there were no nicks on the blade of the *chalif* rending it non-kosher. That's how we lived then. We had no inside heating and no hot or cold water in the house—one of the conveniences that you're used to in America. If you needed cold water, you went to the well and *schleped* it home. If you needed hot water, you boiled the cold water and then you had your hot water.

There were many wells throughout the town. We had one across the street from our house. It was difficult drawing water from the well. You had to lower the bucket on a chain, and then crank it back up again. It was very heavy. Fortunately, there was a gentile who brought water to the house for us. My sister and I only had to draw water when he was sick. The water carriers put a pole over their shoulders with a pail of water at either end. Obviously, we appreciated our water."

Material Life in the Community

"Let me tell you what the town of Kelm looked like. Kelm is located in the northwestern part of Lithuania. The town is surrounded by trees, not like Mir that is surrounded by open fields. The whole town is only a few blocks long and a few blocks wide. There was a *poritz* (squire) who owned the land and forests outside the town. He didn't let us onto his estates, but we could sit by the trees. In the town itself, most people had a little garden called a *mye*, where they grew flowers. It was called a *mye* because everything would start to bloom in May. Some people even had apple trees. We had a country style of living, not like in the countryside in America, it was a much harder way of life, but you get an idea of what it was like by comparison.

We lived in a house made from heavy wood beams, like a log cabin, with thick logs, one on top of the other, and something like cement between them. On top we had a straw roof which kept out the rain and snow. Some people had tin roofs, and one man, a *g'vir*, a very rich man who lived by himself, had a house made from bricks. Some had their own house and some had tenants...one family, maybe two...but not more. We had a little kitchen for cooking, a dining room and two bedrooms. It was a very small house (approximately 312 square feet, with 2 rooms 6' × 12' and two rooms of about 8' × 12'). I remember that it had tiny windows, around 9 to 12 inches wide by 9 to 12 inches high.

The winters in Lithuania were **cold**, around 20 degrees below zero the whole winter, from *Rosh Chodesh Cheshvan* until Purim. After Purim the snow started to melt a little, but until then, through the whole winter, there was ice and snow. There was a big stove in the middle of the house and we heated it by burning wood logs. It had four sides and heated the entire house, but only if you left the doors open to all the rooms. No privacy, right! That's how it was. It was so cold some nights that by morning the water in the house was frozen. You had to hit it with a hammer and then melt the pieces.

The house didn't stay hot all day. We lit the stove first thing in the morning and it was warm until 5 or 6 o'clock in the afternoon, then we relit it and the house was warm again until 11 or 12 o'clock at night. By then we were in bed under our

Rabbi Yisroel Salanter, 1810—1883:

The head of a large company turned to Reb Yisroel Salanter with the following question. He had only one free hour a day to learn. What should he learn during that time? "Spend the hour learning Mussar," answered Reb Yisroel. "If you do so, you will discover many more free hours in the day."

(Sparks of Mussar, page 13)

While living in Memel, Reb Yisroel instituted the practice of lighting the oven in the *Beis Medrash* very early in the morning, so that the wagoners who crossed the border at night would be able to come in and warm themselves.

(Sparks of Mussar, page 25)

Rabbi Simcha Zissel Ziv, 1829—1898:

On *Chol Hamoed* Succos he sang the verses in *Koheles* that begin "Remember your Creator in the days of your youth..." for six consecutive hours.

(Sparks of Mussar, page 65)

"My father," said Reb Nochum Zev Braude in describing Reb Simcha Zissel, "was like a lion-trainer who cannot let his attention wander for a minute lest he be attacked by the lion. Reb Simcha Zissel held on to his emotions and physical desires, and did not let them go for a moment."

(Sparks of Mussar, page 63)

feather blankets...so we were warm, but only as long as we stayed in bed!

During the day we wore sweaters in the house, and if you went outside and your hair was wet or your nose was running, it would freeze! It was *freezing* outside. You can't imagine how we lived then, how everyone lived then: no hot water, no indoor toilets, no central heating and no heat at all during the night. People have to know this, because today we take everything for granted. If you had to go to the bathroom at night, you got dressed and went outside, even if it was 20 degrees below

*The winters in Lithuania were **cold**, around 20 degrees below zero the whole winter, from Rosh Chodesh Cheshvan until Purim.*

'Marktug' (market day) in a small shtetel
in eastern Poland

A view of a small shtetel in eastern Poland

After finishing work at 5 or 6 o'clock in the evening, every ba'al habayis (working man) went to shul. Everyone went to shul! The shoemakers and dressmakers... everyone.

zero...even during a snow storm. In the mornings we put on coats, lit the oven as quickly as possible and then stood around the oven until we warmed up.

We also used the stove for cooking. First you put in logs and lit a fire so that the wood burned down to hot coals. When the coals were ready, you pushed them to the side and put in the food to cook. If you wanted to cook something small, there was a smaller opening with a little door. You put in a *dryfus*, a little tripod, placed the pot on top and wood underneath to cook the food. But this was only for something small. To cook soup, a chicken or *cholent* you used the big oven. You can see a picture of the stove in Ruchama Shain's book about her father.[23]

No one had a telephone in their house, we wrote letters. Today letter writing would be an important lesson in patience, because now people aren't even patient enough to talk to one person at a time, they have a beep so that they can cut off one person to speak with another. What happened to the first person? They aren't important anymore? When I was a child we sometimes waited for months to receive a response to our letters. Can you imagine waiting so long to hear important news about your loved ones? You call someone today and in the middle of a sentence they tell you to wait, disappear, and then come back and tell you they have to go. A *mishagas*?! Also, when I was a child we first started to use light bulbs. A little 15 watt bulb. That's all, no electric appliances to cook with, just a little bulb. Not everyone had bulbs, so you borrowed them for important occasions.

We didn't have a bathtub, and I already told you that there was no running water. To bathe, you had to heat water over the fire and then pour it into a big *shiseleh*, a big pot or tub. The men went to the *mikveh*. It was heated the same way."

Spiritual Life in the Community

"After finishing work at 5 or 6 o'clock in the evening, every *ba'al habayis* (working

---

23. Refer to the book, **ALL FOR THE BOSS**, by Feldheim Publishers, for a picture of such a stove.

man) went to shul. Everyone went to shul! The shoemakers and dressmakers... everyone. Some learned *Mishnayos* and *Shulchan Aruch*. Those who were bigger *lamdonim* learned in the *Chevra Shas*, the *Gemora* group. Some learned the *meforshim* on the *Gemora* as well. There were 22 or 23 men learning in the Kelm Talmud Torah full time, and sometimes as many as 30. The rest of the town worked, but after work everyone went to shul and sat and learned *l'fee darko*, according to his own level.

In *Elul* there were more men learning in the *Talmud Torah* because men who had learned there, and subsequently married and moved away to other towns, came back to sit and learn for the whole month. They left their businesses for their wives to run, and came to learn until after Yom Kippur. They returned home for Succos.

Shabbos was special. On Shabbos everything was closed...all the stores were closed...everything closed. Even the young people who had been influenced by the *maskilim*, the free thinkers, and weren't so religious anymore wouldn't be *m'challel Shabbos* in front of anyone. No one would do that. Some of them would go out of town near the forest to smoke a cigarette, maybe. But nobody saw any such thing in the streets.

On Shabbos my father would never sleep, he didn't lie down the whole day in order not to interrupt his *avodas Hashem*. Even in his 90's he would never lie down during the day. When my mother was old he used to tell her not to lie down because that's when the *malach hamaves* can come and take you. Today you can't say that to someone because people are weaker nowadays. Only when he was sick did he lie down, but otherwise, never! He used to learn.

Rabbi Simcha Zissel Ziv:

When they washed before meals (in the yeshiva), it was customary for every student, after he had washed his hands, to fill the cup with water for the next one.

(Sparks of Mussar, page 79)

Reb Simcha Zissel Ziv once apologized to his friend, Reb Itzele Peterburger, for not writing, explaining that he couldn't afford the postage. His poverty was sometimes so severe that the family's diet consisted of groat porridge. Rain dripped through a hole in the roof of their apartment, which was unheated because they could not afford firewood.

(Sparks of Mussar, page 77)

He was careful never to eat a food for which he had a craving. After fasting, he would eat small bony fish in order to break the desire to eat and to acquire the *midah*, quality, of patience.

(Sparks of Mussar, page 78)

For a while, Reb Simcha Zissel had all the students rise at 3:30 in the morning, eat breakfast, and learn from 4 to 7. The purpose of this schedule was to drill them in the *midah* of zeal and to train them to fix times for learning, even under unusual conditions.

Reb Simcha Zissel also instituted a five-minute *seder*, for which the students were required to come in specially. Its purpose was to accustom them to value time and to concentrate their thoughts quickly.

Shabbos afternoons, he would not let us go outside and play, he didn't want us to be wild. After *shalosh seudos* we had to stay in the house because he felt when Shabbos goes away you have to remove yourself from the outside world. He held that the *neshamah yeseirah*, the extra soul that comes to each Jew on Shabbos, starts to leave at that time and a person should be a little *b'tzar*...a little bit sorrowful. He also felt that a person had to go against what other people are doing, that you didn't have to go along with the crowd. His whole life he fought against his emotions and desires, so that he should rule over them

On Shabbos my father would never sleep, he didn't lie down the whole day in order not to interrupt his avodas Hashem.

Ezrielke the 'Shabbos-klaper' in Baila, Poland. His job was to knock on window shutters to inform everyone that Shabbos was about to begin.

Purim. How one Jewish girl brought about such a salvation, and all that *Chazal* taught about it. The only pretty girl was a Jew? None of the gentile girls were pretty? It was a *nes*, a miracle, that she was chosen. You see that Hashem runs everything, all the details of the world, no matter how small. Purim came at the end of winter so there weren't any fruits available. In summer we had apples, plums, pears and cherries. We didn't have oranges because you had to bring them from warm places. We only had oranges for Purim, for *mishloach manos,* but they were expensive. During the year we also had cocoa and tea.

Pesach was completely different than what it is like here in America. First, the matzoh wasn't ready-made, it was all baked by hand. Everyone had to bake matzoh for themselves. Every town had their own bakery, someone owned the bakery and you paid to use it. I helped to roll out the dough for the matzoh. It wasn't as thin as it is today, it was much thicker and heavier.

Also, everyone had borscht. Around Purim time we prepared a big barrel and put in beets and water, letting the beets sour until Pesach. We also had potatoes, and *knaidelach* that we made from ground matzoh. Oil we didn't have! Chanukah time we cleaned the oven and the *dryfus*, took out some Pesach pots, bought a goose, cut out the fat, and fried it with onions to make *schmaltz* to cook with on *yom tov*. We stored the *schmaltz* in a small closet off the side of the house called an *almer*. It was very cold in the closet and the foods kept perfectly, like a freezer today.

Carrots were hard to find at that time of the year in Europe. The farmers stored them in their basements, deep underground. We bought a few to make *tzimmes* (a carrot and prune dish). Chickens you

and respond only to what Hashem would want him to do, and not what people may have wanted. *Neged hazerem!* Against the flow! He used to go *neged hazerem* throughout his whole life. He was a *tzaddik*...and this is what he taught us. But, in truth, there were many striving to achieve this high level, before Hitler, *yemach sh'mo*.

Purim was a highlight of the year. My father would tell us about the miracles of could buy live in the market. We also made *farfel kugel* from the matzoh. Everything was made from matzos or potatoes or onions. We had *chrein* (horseradish) and gefilte fish, simple things. Fish we bought fresh. Our *sedorim* were the same as today, they were very long. We would have a couple of my father's students for the *Seder* so that he would have a *mezumin* (a quorum of three males) for *Hallel* and *bentching*. Every *erev* Pesach my father checked the house, but we didn't work there like we work here. We didn't have a lot and the house was small, so in three days we cleaned up and were finished.

Everyone was religious when I was a child, but the younger generation had already started to go down in their observance because of the influence of Mendelsshon's[24] teachings. Though they started to become less religious they weren't *prust* (crude) like many young people in America. They were better educated in secular studies, but they were on a different religious level, a higher level, than Jews who are not religious in America.

When I came to America in 1947, there wasn't the *chutzpah* (rudeness) that there is today. Even though there weren't many religious Jews, they weren't spoiled like children are today. In those days children had a *yirah* for their fathers, and *yiras hakavod* for their mothers. In Europe, if a child did something wrong they got a *pahtch* (a spanking) and were put in their room. The same thing in school, if we misbehaved we were put in the corner. We were disciplined and were afraid to misbehave...that's how it was.

There were very few men like my father in his generation. Even in the Kelm Talmud Torah, in his time, there were few like him. Some of the men in the Talmud Torah were in business 2 or 3 hours a day, but most of them learned all day in the yeshiva. My father was a young man in his thirties when we were in Kelm, but he had a *shem*, he had a name. There were others who had a *shem*, but these men were destroyed in the Holocaust. If not for Hitler, *yemach sh'mo*, there would be a lot of *groisa mentschen* now. Europe, in general, had many big *talmidei chachomim*.

> *My father was a young man in his thirties when we were in Kelm, but he had a* shem, *he had a name. There were others who had a* shem, *but these men were destroyed in the Holocaust.*

Jews purchasing beets from a Polish peasant on market day

In Vilna there was Reb Chaim Ozer Grodzenski. He was a very big *chachom*, the leader of his generation, and a *groiser tzaddik*. People would come from all over to see him, to ask for his advice and help. Some went for his *brochos*. For *brochos*, however, people would usually go to the Chafetz Chaim in Radin. There were plenty of great people in Europe...in Telz, Slonim, Lvov, Kletzk, Kaminetz, Lodz, Novardok, Lublin, Ponevezh, Satmar, Bobov, Bialistock, Brisk, Kobrin, Volozhin, Kovno...plenty of great people, but Hitler destroyed them. Not just the famous *Roshei Yeshiva*, there were many, many great *talmidim* also...great in learning, in righteousness...but they're all gone now. Hitler destroyed them all...he destroyed a civilization that existed for over a thousand years. It's all gone now...gone...all gone. You're talking to me, why not talk to the Rebbetzins from Telz, they'll tell you what it was like. Talk to the *Chasidim* from Slonim, from Bobov, from Satmar... they'll tell you what it was like before Hitler, *yemach sh'mo*.

To know what a loss we suffered you had to have lived in Europe before the war— to see the piety of the simple Jew, a holiness handed down

A Jew in Zarki, Poland being taunted as he recites Kaddish *over murder victims of the Nazis*

from generation to generation, parent to child. In my father's case (and those of other great and simple Jews who survived the war) he became very great after everything he went through, because he lived to grow older. However, even at a very young age he was a special example of what the *Talmud Torah mentchin* were like. Torah, closeness to Hashem, striving to become great in *avodas Hashem*, that's what it was like in the Kelm Talmud Torah...and in the yeshivos of Poland and Lithuania. That's not how it was for everyone before the war, however, for there were many, many Jews who had strayed

far away from a Torah life. I always say that if a person lives to an old age, and has learned Torah all his life, then people will come to him for blessings

I'll tell you a little story about my father. My mother had a brother in America, and when World War I ended my uncle wanted to help us, so he sent us fifty American dollars in the mail. My father didn't want to take the money because he was afraid that my uncle worked on Shabbos. It was a custom of the Kelm Talmud Torah not to take such money. He wrote to my uncle inquiring if he worked on Shabbos. My uncle wrote back and said that in America you can't live without working on Shabbos.[25] In those days the mailman would give all the letters to one of the people on the street to deliver to the rest of the neighbors. One of my uncles obtained the letter in this way, and when he saw what my other uncle wrote he changed the letter so that it said that he did keep Shabbos. He did this so that my father would be able to use the money.

The whole *Chodesh Elul* my father accepted a *taanis dibur.* He didn't speak. All his life, I think, was a *taanis dibur.* But in *Elul* if he had something to say, if he needed to tell my mother something, or say something about the children, he wrote it on a piece of paper: "Please may I have bread, please bring me the sugar..." This is how he conducted himself the whole month. The rest of the year he would speak, no *loshon hora* (forbidden speech), but he would speak.

In general, throughout Eastern Europe during the month of *Elul* most everyone was very, very serious. My father certainly was. He taught us that on Rosh Hashanah we have to stand before the Creator and try to be *zocheh b'din,* so we have to prepare ourselves. If a person has to go to court, before the date arrives he is very aggravated and anxious, thinking only about the court case. He doesn't waste time thinking about little things. He prepares himself to stand before the judge and jury. We, also, have to prepare ourselves to stand before the Judge, the real Judge, so we need to think in this same manner. We have the whole month of *Elul* to prepare ourselves to be better. The whole *Chodesh Elul* was very, very hard.

In addition, the Three Weeks and from *Rosh Chodesh Av* until after *Tisha b'Av* were very difficult. We were *mitzayer* ourselves, we afflicted ourselves emotionally, over the *churban Bais Hamikdash.* We used to learn about it, and talk about it...and think about *Moshiach.* You don't see many people like this now.

Erev Rosh Hashanah my father would not talk or write at all. He was very solemn and reflective, he understood that it was a very grave and perilous time. He learned a lot of *mussar* the day before Rosh Hashanah. He stood in prayer for a long time on the *Yomim Noraim.* His *talmidim* did this as well. They didn't necessarily accept upon themselves a *taanis dibur,* but they were fearful of Hashem's awesome judgment on Rosh Hashanah. It was like that in all of the yeshivos...in Mir and in Kletzk.

A *chasunah* in Europe was very different as well. The days leading up to the *chasunah* were days of *yirah* (awe) very much different than in America. The day of the *chasunah* itself was one of great solemnity, both the *choson* and *kallah* felt

In general, throughout Eastern Europe during the month of Elul most everyone was very, very serious.

Rebbetzin Zlota Ginsburg Collection

*Our engagement photo
(Rabbi Ephraim Mordechai Ginsburg and Miss Zlota Levenstein)*

25. There are several books available describing the sacrifices that many Orthodox Jews made in order to properly observe Shabbos in the first half of the 20th century in America. Among others, the reader is referred to **All For The Boss,** Feldheim Publishers, and **The Way It Was,** Mesorah Publications.

Rebbetzin Zlota Ginsburg Collection

Our "Chasunah" photo
(Rabbi & Rebbetzin Ephraim Mordechai Ginsburg)

One picture, that's all. At the *chasunah* itself my father would never, never let pictures be taken. He would never allow such a thing! He used to say that flowers is a *goyishe minhag*, pictures as well.

In Europe you didn't give money as a present at a *chasunah*. You gave a towel, bedding, a tablecloth, but not money. When I went to my first *chasunah* in America, they told us you give a present of money. What? Money? You have to pay? You have to pay for the meal and give money? We were all laughing. You have to pay for the food, for the meal? What kind of *mishagas* is that? America! When the *bochurim* from America came to the Mir to learn and brought pictures of *chasunahs* in America we used to laugh because it was like a *goyishe chasunah* in Europe. That's a *chasunah*?

Let me describe to you what our *chasunahs* were like. Before the *chuppah*, the *choson* was in one house and the *kallah* was in another. At the *kabbolas ponim* in the house of the *choson* the men would say *divrei Torah*, and by the *kallah*, the ladies would have cake, cookies, fruit, light refreshments. Then the *unterfherers*, two men chosen for this honor, would bring the *choson* to the *kallah* for the *badecking*. The *chuppah* would take place next to the shul, under the open sky. First came the *choson*, but not with his parents. The *unterfherers* would walk the *choson* to the *chuppah*, and then two women would bring the *kallah*, again, not her parents.

I remember that my cousin wanted her *chuppah* next to her house, also under the sky, because she didn't want everyone to see her being escorted to the shul. She wanted my father and mother to be the *unterfherers*, but my father said no, that it's not *mazaldik* to change the way the ceremony is conducted, it won't bring good fortune. It wasn't good, they

> *The day of my chasunah I fasted and knew it was Yom Kippur, that I could make everything in my life better that day...I could become much closer to Hashem.*

this way. They would cry under the *chuppah*. The day of my *chasunah* I fasted and *knew* it was Yom Kippur, that I could make everything in my life better that day...I could become much closer to Hashem. In America everything is a joke! A *chasunah* is what kind of food you are going to serve, what kind of band will it be, what kind of flowers are you going to have. There we had nothing— no flowers, no pictures...nothing. You see this *chasunah* picture of me, do you know that it was taken after the *chasunah*! My husband and I got dressed up again and had the picture taken *(on left)*.

went to America and went off the *derech*. My father was right, It wasn't *mazaldik*.

Only close friends came to a *chasunah* in the small towns. Even to a *levayah* and to be *menachem avel* not everyone came. Not like here where it's a convention with people laughing and discussing different topics. When we went to be *menachem avel* we only talked about the *niftar* and nothing else. The *avel* would tell stories about the *niftar,* and the people were sitting and talking about the *niftar*. It was a different life...more *kodesh*, more holy.

We didn't have many possessions. I had two weekday dresses for the winter and one for Shabbos, and two weekday dresses for the summer and one for Shabbos. We didn't have birthday parties when I was child...you didn't receive gifts. You had only what you needed, there wasn't extra money for luxuries. Many times, in the cities and towns of Lithuania and Poland, there wasn't enough money for food. Between the two world wars the Polish Parliament passed many, many laws that, on the surface, were not anti-Semitic, but were aimed at crippling the ability of Jews to own a business and make a living, and they were very effective."[26]

Youth and Education in the Community

"The men of the *Talmud Torah* made a school for girls called Shulamis. The school was started by Rabbi Yisroel Stamm (a Rov and communal leader for three decades in Lithuania, who eventually moved to Eretz Yisrael and was *nifter* in Bnei Brak). I was a student in Shulamis from age 7 until I was 12. We learned everything in the school: all of *Tanach* (Torah, Prophets and Writings) and Hebrew as well. All the subjects were

taught in Hebrew, but we only spoke Yiddish at home. Lithuanian was the language in Kelm, like English is spoken in America. The teachers were from the Slobodka Yeshiva. Like one who goes to work here to make a living, some of the men from Slobodka came to teach us in Kelm. Slobodka was to the south of us, closer to Poland. There was a lady who came to teach us from Telz. In Telz, there were

---

Rabbi Simcha Zissel Ziv:

When the *shamas* came to call him for *Ma'ariv* of Rosh Hashanah, Reb Simcha Zissel would be seized with trembling and fear, and would mutter in fright, "The summons to court has arrived!"
(Sparks of Mussar, page 70)

Shabbos evening upon returning from Ma'ariv, he would pause for a while in the entrance of his home to study all the Shabbos preparations. He would observe the beautifully set table and the many delicious foods in order to be properly grateful to his wife, who had gone to so much trouble for him.
(Sparks of Mussar, pages 69-70)

On Mussar:
He accepted upon himself to devote every tenth day from Yom Kippur on to character building. He would leave all his other affairs and concentrate solely on spiritual perfection. He would carefully weigh all his behavior toward G-d or man and undertake various Mussar actions, such as refraining from speaking, to correct his *Midos*.
(Sparks of Mussar, page 66)

"The Chofetz Chaim" Rabbi Yisroel Meir HaKohen 1839—1933:

Reb Yisroel Meir did various exercises to prepare for the services in the Temple that, as a *Kohen*, he would be required to perform when the *Moshiach* comes. He prepared a special garment in which to greet the *Moshiach*.
(Sparks of Mussar, page 251)

---

26. See interview with Mr. Yosef Friedenson in **The World That Was: Poland** / Section 2, page 124.

"Der Alter of Slobodka" Rabbi Nosson Tzvi Finkel, 1849—1927:

The Alter treated his wife in the most noble manner. He tried to shield her from sorrow and trouble, and he helped her in the house. Even so, on *erev* Yom Kippur, before he left for the yeshiva, he would beg her forgiveness lest he had not acted toward her with adequate respect. If he felt that she was hesitant in granting it, he would tremble all over. He would not leave the house, although the yeshiva was waiting for him, until she expressly stated that she forgave him with all her heart.

(Sparks of Mussar, pages 156-157)

He (Rav Chatzkel) felt that the husband should be the head of the family and that if the wife knows as much or more, there could be trouble in the marriage, since the wife may feel equal to her husband.

two teacher's training seminaries, one for men and one women, started by the Telzer Rov and Rosh HaYeshiva, Rabbi Yosef Leib Bloch.[27] In fact, we had a few teachers from Telz.

Not everyone in Kelm went to the Shulamis school. Some went to the Tzeirei Tzion school, where boys and girls learned together. On Shabbos some of the boys would go out to the fields to play ball. There was a *groiser tzaddik* named Reb Zelig Tarshish in Kelm. He used to wear *tallis* and *tefillin* all day long while learning in a shul. His wife had a store and they lived on the money she earned. On Shabbos he would go for a walk in the fields and when the boys would see him they would immediately stop playing ball. They were showing him respect. *Derech eretz* was something we had even for strangers, not like here in America where some children don't have *derech eretz* for their parents. In Europe, even a child who was not so religious showed *derech eretz* for his parents.

Sara Schenirer had some initial difficulty starting her seminary because until then the girls' schools were for younger girls, 11 or 12 years of age, and she wanted to start a school for older girls, 16-18 years of age (it was a two year program).

My father didn't let us go because he felt if a girl was too educated she wouldn't want a *ben Torah* for a husband, that she may not respect him as much if she received a wider, somewhat secular education. He felt that the husband should be the head of the family and that if the wife knows as much or more, there could be trouble in the marriage, since the wife may feel equal to her husband. Also, he didn't feel that the wife should be the main supporter of the family.

He changed when he came to Eretz Yisrael; then he told my sister to send her daughter to Bais Yaakov, because a woman had to help support her husband learn.

I think that a lot of the divorces today are because the wife thinks she is the equal of her husband. The Torah says that the husband should rule in the house— *v'hu yimshal bah*, "...and he shall rule over her." You think that everybody lived so happily in Europe? My father said that 25% of the couples were perfectly happy, 50% were half and half, and the other 25% were not happy. However, a woman had nowhere to go, no welfare, nothing. If there was a *get,* a divorce, there was nothing but hardship for her and the family.

My father taught that you cannot go against the Torah, therefore, should the woman be more educated than the man, and support him, she may end up feeling superior to him. Why do you see so much trouble in America today, because

---

27. See section on Telz, page 22.

women don't want *v'hu yimshal bah*, they want to be equals. I'm not saying my own thoughts, I'm saying Torah. Another problem about attending Bais Yaakov was the expense. Very few people had the money to send a girl away to Cracow, it was a big expense to send a child away like that."

The Role of the Family in the Community

"My father was born in Warsaw, but he first learned in Lomza, then Radin, and finally he came to Kelm. I was never in Radin, and when I grew up the Chafetz Chaim had already died. You see, we didn't marry so young. There weren't many rich people to support a boy in learning for any length of time after he married, so the men married late. The girls married at 21 or 22 and the boys at 27 or 28. After marriage it was very hard. There weren't

kollelim then, maybe in all of Poland there were two *kollelim*. After marriage the men lived in their father-in-law's house and learned for a year or two, but after a couple of children they had to go out and earn a living: fix watches, open or work in a dry goods store, become *shochtim, maggidim* or *chazonim,* everybody did something. Some received positions as *rabbonim*. If a boy married a girl whose father was a *Rov*, he took over the position when his father-in-law died. Today, if a boy is 25 he's considered old.

My father had two sisters and a brother in Warsaw, but they were all killed in the war. It seems that Hitler killed everybody. My father was 5-years-old when his mother died. His father remarried and his stepmother had two sons. One was a businessman, and the other was sent to us to learn in Kelm, but he didn't want to learn. The stepmother sent him right after his Bar Mitzvah and he stayed with my parents until he was 17 or 18. He went back to Warsaw during World War I and was drafted into the Polish army and was killed in the war. The other brother and sisters were killed by Hitler.

My paternal grandfather was a Gerrer *chassid*, a *frumer yid,* but he wanted my father to learn a business, so he put him to work in a store. He worked a couple of years, but then he remembered that before his mother died she had called him to her sickbed and told him that she wanted him to *bleib* in learning (Torah). Honoring her wish, he left the business and went to learn. His

Yeshiva bochurim on Nalewki Street in Warsaw, 1928

There weren't many rich people to support a boy in learning for any length of time after he married, so the men married late. The girls married at 21 or 22 and the boys at 27 or 28.

*The Gerrer Rebbe,
Rabbi Avraham Mordechai Alter*

mother was a *bas chassidim,* in fact, her father was a *Rebbe.* My father told me that, "my mother said by the *Kisay Hakoved* (Hashem's holy throne) that she wants me to learn." Can you imagine saying that to a 5-year-old today? He remembered and listened. First he went to a Polish yeshiva, Markov, for a while, and then to Lomza. In Lomza he slept on a bench and ate his meals by various families because he didn't have any money. Remember, his father didn't want him to do this, he wanted him to remain in business. When he came to Radin the yeshiva gave him money for expenses, but he was very poor. His sister sent him a few zlotys after she was married, but he really had nothing but Torah.

There is an interesting story told about my father that I will tell to you. After work one *Erev Shabbos* he went to the *mikveh.* While getting dressed to leave he found that his wages for the week had been stolen.

He felt that if this is what can happen to all one's efforts in this world, then he wants to learn Torah, where one's efforts are his forever. Personally, I don't believe this story. Maybe he told this to someone, but in my house I never heard it! I only know that he always told us that his mother wanted him to learn Torah, so he left work and went to learn Torah. Maybe he told one of his students this story, this I can't tell you. They are telling stories about him that I know nothing about. Miracles and wonders that he did or that happened to him. You think I know everything? However, this I *can* tell you, he had *Ruach Hakodesh,* this I know. He had *Ruach Hakodesh* in his older age...no, not only in his older age, even when he was younger. When we were in Shanghai, China, during World War II he was the Mirrer *Mashgiach.* At that time Shanghai was at war with Japan, and America was at war with Japan. Everyone was afraid that the Americans would bomb Shanghai, which they did. There were many older *bochurim* with us in Shanghai, like Rabbi Leib Malin from Bais HaTalmud, and some of them came to my father advising him that we should leave Shanghai because the city is a strategic point, and the Americans will surely bomb it. They wanted to go to a small city in another part of China. My father replied that in no way would he allow such a move, but he didn't tell the *talmidim* the reason. The previous night his *rebbeim* came to him in a dream and told him not to leave Shanghai because here he would be safe; and so it was.

I lost a child after we reached America, a boy 9-years-old. My father and mother were in Eretz Yisrael at the time and when my son died I didn't want to tell them. So we asked Reb Nochum Partzovitz (the future Mirrer Rosh HaYeshiva in Jerusalem) to tell him. When Reb Nochum came

Reb Nochum Partzovitz,
Mirrer Rosh HaYeshiva *in Jerusalem*

to my father and told him that he had some news that was not so good, my father responded that he already knew. Reb Nochum asked how he knew that the child had died. My father revealed that he had seen his father and his rebbe burying the child in a dream. The child was named after both of them, my grandfather's name was Yehuda, and my father's rebbe was Reb Hirsch Braude, the son-in-law of the Alter from Kelm, and the child was named Yehuda Hirsch. I know that many of the older *gedolim* had things revealed to them in such a manner.

My husband also knew when his time came. He had a heart attack the first year we were in Brooklyn after leaving Shanghai. The doctor said it was from the *tzores* of living in Shanghai. He lived 12 more years after that attack. He took a vacation to get away from the heat of the city, so that people wouldn't say that it was because of the heat that he died. He never went on a vacation, but this time he did...he knew he would not come back. He had

a dream that he would die, and he went to Reb Hirsch Feldman, the *Mashgiach* of the Mirrer Yeshiva (Brooklyn, NY) to be *poser cholom,* (interpret his dream). Reb Hirsch told me this after he died, that my husband saw what would happen in a dream, but he didn't want to tell me. There were many great people before the war, and many who became great because of the war."

Jews and Gentiles in the Community

"Poland is a very, very bad country. The Polish people didn't have to pay taxes for their animals, but the Jews had to pay taxes for their stores.[28] They made a decree that

28. See interview with Mr. Yosef Friedenson in **The World That Was: Poland** / Section 2, page 129.

the Jews could not *shecht* their animals. The Chofetz Chaim, who was very old at the time, went to Warsaw to seek an audience with the President of Poland. The great *tzaddik* explained to him that the way a Jew kills an animal is more humane than how the gentiles kill their animals, that it is an easier way for the animal to die. He won the case.

What I am going to tell you now is very important: you have to appreciate that America is a country of *tzedakah*. The government could give money to all the minorities, but tell the yeshiva boys: "you have to go to work! There's no money for Jews!" This is why Hashem is good to America, because America helps the Jews as well. The countries of the world look up to America because it is a country of *tzedakah*. To the minorities and elderly America should give, but you have to appreciate that many Torah institutions also receive generous aid from the government. The yeshivas get a good deal of support from government programs. This is a country of kindness, and I think that America has a portion in Torah because of the government support that helps Jews to learn Torah. No country in Europe gave like America, not even Germany. Who are the judges in America? Who is giving advice to the President? Many are Jews, right? Because the Jews are the *Am Hanivchar,* the nation to whom Hashem gave *chochmah.* What could you do if the government officials would cut off all aid?

The "Chofetz Chaim"–Rabbi Yisroel Meir HaKohen

That's how it was in Europe, the yeshivas didn't receive government aid. To the contrary, the Jews and the yeshivas were harassed by the government. But here, in America, there are programs which offer support to those who are learning...and yet there are still some people who complain about America.

I tell you to go to Poland and Europe and see what they give the Jews. How much do they love the Jews now that communism is over? All over Europe there is nationalism and anti-Semitism, you don't see that from the American government. How many Jews do the *goyim* think are left in Europe? Millions? They killed most of them! Don't they remember? It worries me that young Jews are going to Russia and Poland, American Jews don't know how evil these people are. How they killed Jewish women and children, and crushed the heads of babies with their rifle butts right in front of their mothers. People who lived through it know how wicked they are. I think you put yourself in danger when you go to these places. If it is so good in these countries, why are the Jews running away now that they can finally get out? Because they are running for their lives, the gentiles there can come to your house and kill you. Talk to the Russian Jews about the anti-Semitism in Russia. If a person needs a vacation, has he seen everything in America that he needs to go to the lands of these murderers? You can read a hundred books, but if you actually lived through the experiences of 50 years ago you *know*. I am thankful that my children and grandchildren listen to me. Those who go to Russia and Eastern Europe to start yeshivas, *shaluchei mitzvah ainon nizokin (one who goes to perform a mitzvah is protected from misfortune),* Hashem will watch them."

Mir, Danzig and Kletzk

"Reb Yeruchem Levovitz, the famous Mirrer *Mashgiach*, wanted to come to Lithuania to be *Mashgiach* in a yeshiva

Reb Yeruchem Levovitz the Mirrer Mashgiach

like Kelm or Ponevezh. So for a little while, when Reb Yeruchem was away, my father was *Mashgiach* in the Mir. While he was there we remained in Kelm. Mir was a very small yeshiva with young boys 17 or 18 years of age, but I don't know exactly how many *talmidim* were there at that time. Since Lithuania and Poland were in a state of war, my father couldn't mail a letter directly to us. There was no telephone, but there was an organization in Germany that helped Jews in Poland and Lithuania. He would mail a letter to the organization and

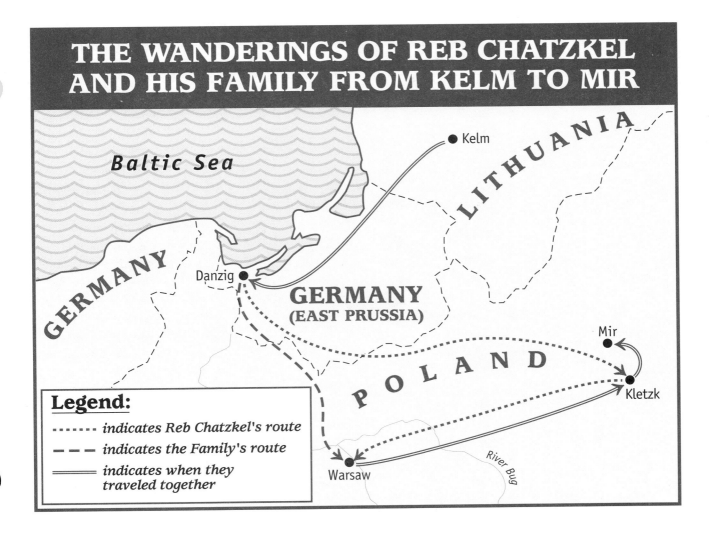

THE WANDERINGS OF REB CHATZKEL AND HIS FAMILY FROM KELM TO MIR

Baltic Sea

Kelm

LITHUANIA

GERMANY

Danzig

GERMANY (EAST PRUSSIA)

Mir

POLAND

Kletzk

Warsaw

River Bug

Legend:
...... *indicates Reb Chatzkel's route*
‒ ‒ ‒ *indicates the Family's route*
═══ *indicates when they traveled together*

Reb Aharon Kotler, Rosh HaYeshiva of Kletzk and then of Lakewood

was sick…so he didn't take the position. He turned down Reb Aharon Kotler's offer because of my *Bubby*. I want to ask you, who would turn down such a position because of a mother-in-law? But he didn't go. She had another daughter in Kelm and a son in Lita, but he didn't go. He stayed in Kelm for three years until after she passed away. I want to tell you how he took care of her— even more than my mother. Every morning he used to come to her and wash her hands for *negel vasser*, and bring her a little cake and wine because he said it would give her strength. Every night he would put away all the knives and such things in the house because he said that after 80 a person can get disoriented and she might hurt herself. She wasn't disoriented, but he wanted to be careful."

Smuggled into Poland

"After *Bubby* passed away my father took us to Danzig, which was a free city (1919-1935), where whoever wanted to enter could do so without restriction. He rented a furnished apartment for us, and for two months tried to arrange papers so that we could enter Poland legally, but he wasn't successful. He had a Polish passport because he was born in Warsaw, and after all these years he had a passport from Lithuania as well, so he had two passports. If he was caught in one country with the passport from the other country he could have been shot, or imprisoned, but he hid whichever passport he didn't need. Now he was in Kletzk and we were in Danzig, but he wasn't successful in securing documents for us.

He traveled to Warsaw where his brother, two sisters and stepmother lived, to seek advice. My father was not so healthy, and he was concerned whether he was strong enough to smuggle us across himself.

Every morning he used to come to her and wash her (his mother-in-law's) hands for negel vasser, and bring her a little cake and wine because he said it would give her strength.

they would forward it to us. My mother would write back and send her letter to the organization to forward to my father. In the meantime, Reb Yeruchem didn't get the position he wanted and wrote my father he was returning to Mir. Reb Aharon Kotler (founder of the Lakewood Yeshiva and one of the main forces behind the growth of Orthodox Judaism in America) knew that my father was leaving Mir, so they spoke together and made up that my father would come to his yeshiva in Kletzk (then in Poland and now in Russia) to assume the position of *Mashgiach*.

Now he had to come home to work out a plan to bring the family out of Lithuania because he didn't want to go to Kletzk alone. My *Bubby* (on my mother's side) was old and couldn't travel. In addition, we didn't have passports to go from Lithuania to Poland because the countries had no diplomatic relations, so we would have to skip the border and be smuggled in. My father wouldn't leave my *Bubby* behind, she was over 80-years-old and she

The Blick auf Synagogue of Danzig—destroyed by the Nazis in 1940

His brother Moshe was younger and healthy, and agreed that he would take us across the border from Danzig into Poland. My uncle hired two gentiles to guide us over the border. He didn't know the way himself, in general the *Yidden* didn't know the way out, so he hired the guides. They didn't carry any weapons, at least no guns. They were only there to show the way.

It was in the middle of the night when they brought us to a place along the border where there were no guards. We didn't talk the whole time. I was 13-years-old and my sister was only 9, so what did we know about these things? I wasn't afraid, I just listened and kept quiet, but my mother was afraid. It wasn't so bad for me, but let me tell you what happened. It was winter time when we left, in the month of *Shevat*, and there was still snow everywhere. My boots were okay, but my sister's boots were no good, and she was practically walking barefoot— as if she had no shoes. She suffered because of this for a long time. They told us not to talk, no talking...only silence. We walked the whole

night, from 10:00pm until 6:00am the next morning. Once we crossed the border no one asked us for a passport because we were inside the country already. We left on a Thursday night and Friday morning we came to a little town to get the train to Warsaw.

We arrived in Warsaw right before Shabbos. I remember when we came, my step-*bubby* and my father... everyone was dancing with us because we didn't get caught. If we would have been caught, the guards would have sent us back, but they would have shot my uncle thinking he was a spy.

After Shabbos we went to Kletzk with my father. We took nothing with us from Kelm, we left everything behind. Can you imagine doing this at such a young age? To leave everything and run away in the middle of the night: pictures, clothes, bedding, pots, pans, everything was left behind.

We owned our house in Kelm, but my father sold the house when he took us to Kletzk. We were still in Danzig when the house was sold. He gave the money to

We arrived in Warsaw right before Shabbos. I remember when we came, my step-bubby and my father... everyone was dancing with us because we didn't get caught.

the Kelm Talmud Torah to erect a new building. They were going to invest it and send us interest from the investment. Then, when we would need the money back, they would return the original investment to us. My mother wasn't happy with that arrangement because she felt that the yeshiva might not have the money to reimburse us when we would need it. But my father was a *tzaddik* and he gave the money to help the yeshiva. He sold the house for 1,200 American dollars, which was a great deal of money at that time. The person investing for the yeshiva promised to send interest checks at certain times, while my father figured he would have the original investment for our dowries: $600.00 for my dowry and the other $600.00 for my sister.

But the war broke out and the Germans took everything away...so we lost the money in the end. Although until the war the man did send dividend checks...sometimes yes, sometimes no, but it was very hard for us to get the money because he had to send it from Lithuania, through Germany, and into Poland. When the Second World War started, and we fled to Vilna, we had nothing but a little bit of the interest money that had been sent to us."

Business courtyard inside the Jewish Quarter in Warsaw, 1938

Roman Vishniac

Kletzk

"Kletzk was a small town, a little bigger than Kelm, but very much the same: no running water and no inside plumbing or heating. Lithuania...Poland...it was all the same. The town was surrounded by forests and the gentiles lived in the little villages and farms surrounding the town. All the towns and villages in Poland and Lithuania were the same. It was only the big cities that were different. Cities like Lodz, Warsaw and Vilna already had inside heating and plumbing. My father remained as *Mashgiach* with Reb Aharon for three years. After that we moved back to Mir where he sat and learned for three and a half years. He had no job then, he just learned.

When my father first came to Kletzk there was no yeshiva building, so the *talmidim* learned in a *Beis Medrash*. He suggested that they acquire a building of their own because a yeshiva needs its own *makom,* but there was no money. So they announced their intention to build a *makom* for the yeshiva, and everyone from the town came with donations: money, bracelets, rings, silver pieces, gold pieces, whatever they had they gave. It was like the offerings of the Jews in the *midbar* for the building of the *Mishkon*. With this money the yeshiva bought a plot of land and held a groundbreaking ceremony.

It was a few years until the building was finished, finally it was completed the last year we were there, but my father had already left for the Mir. We remained in Kletzk until he settled everything in Mir. When he returned to spend Pesach and bring us back to Mir, the building was finished and there was a beautiful *Chanukas Habayis* (ceremony honoring the dedication of the new yeshiva building).

It seemed like every Rov in Poland came— the Pinsker Rov, the Slonimer Rov, the Baranovich Rov, the Yankelpolaner Rov...all the *rabbonim* from the cities and towns around Kletzk came. Not from places that were far away like Warsaw, but some of the *rabbonim* from Galicia came and many of the Polish *rabbonim* were there. The *Roshei Yeshiva* and *bochurim* from the Mir came as well. It was a very big ceremony.

In Kletzk there was no religious schooling for girls, only for the boys. There was something like a public school where the girls went, and at night a teacher gave them lessons in *Tanach*. My father didn't want my sister and me to go to public school, so he hired a private teacher who instructed us in Polish, which we didn't know because we were from Lithuania. We also

During construction to complete a new 'makom' for the Yeshiva in Kletzk

Inside the new yeshiva's Beis Hamedrash, 1939

learned German and mathematics. He taught us *Tanach* himself. My father liked the study of science, and we learned a lot of science in elementary school, but in Kletzk we didn't because it was another subject and each subject cost money, so it was too expensive. Anyway, I could read, so I could get books and teach myself science.

We had two close friends in Kletzk. The population was *frum*, but a little bit

"The Ohr Yechezkel"
Rabbi Yechezkel Levenstein
1885—1974:

"...for His kindness is forever." The kindness of Hashem Yisborach is not just for a short period of time, rather, it is given forever. Hashem bestows His kindness upon a person according to the depth and sincerity of one's *Emunah*—one's belief and faith in Hashem. Therefore, a person is obligated to constantly strive to gain greater and greater levels of *Emunah,* in order to constantly draw forth and receive the kindness of The Holy One, may He be Blessed.

(Sefer Emunah, page 188.)

A person should discipline himself in all situations to trust and rely on *Hashem Yisborach,* for then Hashem will certainly help him. We must understand that all difficulties are only tests to see if we will be strong, and in the face of all obstacles, truly trust in Hashem.   *(Page 129)*

You see, the whole situation was very bad in Poland then, no one really had parnosah... *For Shabbos we had one chicken for 4 people for 2 meals, an eighth of a chicken per meal per person, and that was from a small chicken.*

modern...the girls went to a public school. My father wanted us to associate with the *yeshivish* people, the girls who would want a *ben Torah* for a husband. I think that this was very much on his mind. During my years in Kletzk everyone in the town was *Shomer Shabbos*, but the girls who went to public school learned different things and had different teachers, we just didn't have that much in common with them.

The girls we were close with didn't survive Hitler, but before the war their fathers were *frum balabatim,* religious men who worked and learned. This is who my father wanted us to be friends with, and we listened. We always listened to my father. My father once told us that a person shouldn't worry if he gets proper *kovod* or not, because Hashem knows the truth, and that's all that matters. We were upset once that he didn't get the honor he deserved, but he told us that Hashem knows, that a person shouldn't lose his *midos* because of such a thing. We were

upset, but he said this is how it is, and that's all there was to it . If he said it, then that's how it was. We listened when my father spoke. He was a *tzaddik.*"

Finances, Learning and Marriage in the Community

"Our house in Kletzk was like the one in Kelm. We had 2 bedrooms...the same thing, 2 girls so there were 2 bedrooms. It was like the bungalows in the country, but built from logs. Just like in Kelm, straw roof and all. But we didn't enjoy the time we spent there because we had very little *parnosah.* You see, the whole situation was very bad in Poland then, no one really had *parnosah.* The people in Poland were very poor, they used to wait for people to come from America, like in Eretz Yisrael today...they used to wait for financial help from relatives in America.

We really didn't have anyone in America...my mother had a brother there, but we didn't have a relationship with him. We just didn't have any money. Our diet consisted of bread, butter and eggs...getting food wasn't so terrible, but to buy clothing was very hard. Food we had, but not candy, chocolate or a good drink— this we didn't have! Only the basics: eggs, bread, butter and meat. In Eastern Europe it was different, meat was cheap and chicken was expensive. Chicken was only for Shabbos. We had meat during the weekdays. When you bought a big order of meat they gave you a piece of liver for nothing and bones were also free, but chicken was very expensive. For Shabbos we had one chicken for 4 people for 2 meals, an eighth of a chicken per meal per person, and that was from a small chicken. My mother would bake *challah* for Shabbos, she baked everything herself.

In those days you didn't have stores to buy shoes, you had to go to a shoemaker

Bochurim in Kletzk crowding in to listen to a shiur given by Reb Aharon

and he measured your feet so that he could make you a proper pair of shoes. Shoes were expensive then. A pair of shoes cost 12 zlotys, about two dollars. It doesn't sound like much now, but then it was a lot of money.

You could make Pesach with ten dollars. A whole Pesach for only $10.00! A family needed about 30 zlotys a week, about five dollars. Of course, it depended on the size of the family. We had a small family.

When a *talmid* came from America to learn at the Mir, he usually took a private rebbe, because the American *bochurim* (and some from Germany and Belgium) were not as well learned as the European *talmidim*. There were not many yeshivas in America then, only Rabbi Yitzchak Elchonon and Torah Vodaath, but they weren't on the same level of learning as the yeshivas in Europe. Boys from *frum*

homes in America would come and pay a *bochur* to learn with them first *seder* and another *bochur* for the second *seder*. Usually they would hire a better *bochur* for the first *seder*. This *bochur* would get ten dollars a month and the second *bochur* would get five dollars a month. The *talmidim* were thrilled to earn so much. They used this money to have a suit made, to buy shoes— for their personal needs. There were no ready-made suits either, you had to have them made. You bought the material and had a tailor make you a suit.

Most of the European *talmidim* received little or nothing in way of support from home. The *Roshei HaYeshiva* used to give them *chalukah,* a stipend, to pay for their room and board. If a *bochur* needed a suit and the family could not afford to buy one for him, he would get money from the *T'aT*, the Tomchei Torah Fund

There were no ready-made suits either, you had to have them made. You bought the material and had a tailor make you a suit.

(Supporters of Torah Fund). You have to understand that people lived in poverty, they just didn't have money.

The *talmidim* in Mir came from all over Europe. They found room and board in the town because there was no dormitory or kitchen in the yeshiva. The Americans usually had money to pay for their expenses, but the Europeans received money from the yeshiva for meat and bread, and some *chalukah* for living expenses. It was about 12 zlotys a month, depending on the boy— an older or better *bochur* would get more. So the boys paired up and rented a room together.

Because there weren't any *kollelim,* married men didn't receive any money from the yeshiva. They worked as a *rebbe* in a Talmud Torah and earned some money by teaching, or they did something else. Sometimes their wives opened a little store and from that they would live while the husband learned. The married men usually had to work and learn, but not the yeshiva *bochurim*. They didn't have people who were working and learning in the Mir, only the *bochurim*. It was like that in all the yeshivas. If a man wanted to learn after he married his father-in-law had to help.

Most of the *talmidim* in the Mir weren't married in Mir, they were married in other towns where there weren't any yeshivas. Every town had a Talmud Torah, but not every town had a yeshiva. The boys would study in the Talmud Torah until bar mitzvah and then go to a *Yeshiva K'tana* for boys 14 and 15-years-old. It was something like a high school, but in Europe there was no high school, classes after bar mitzvah were called

Rav Shmuel Berenbaum— Mirrer Rosh HaYeshiva in Brooklyn, NY

a *yeshiva k'tana*. To go to a *yeshiva gedolah* you went to Radin, Kletzk, Mir, Telz, Ponevezh. Even in Baranovich, Rov Elchonon Wasserman didn't have a *yeshiva gedolah*, his oldest *talmidim* were 16 or 17-years-old, maybe 18. Then they would go to Kletzk, or Kaminetz to Reb Boruch Ber, or to Grodno to Reb Shimon Shkop. Many men learned for 10 years, and there were some men who remained in learning for even longer periods of time before they married."

Mir

"I left Kletzk when I was 17-years-old. My father stayed in Mir for three years, until he went to Petach Tikvah. Mir was a small town of about 700 families, a little bigger then Kelm, but smaller then Kletzk. Those years at the Mir we really didn't have much to live on.

Most people in Mir didn't make a living from business, they made money by taking care of the yeshiva *bochurim*. There were about 500 boys learning in the yeshiva at that time, but there was no dormitory or kitchen, so the *talmidim* used to eat by their landlady. Some ladies rented rooms and also cooked meals, some just cooked meals and some just rented rooms. That brought in some income, and some people also worked as *sofrim* (scribes) to bring in a little more *parnosah* (income). They would write *Sifrei Torah* and send them to America.

The *bochurim* came from cities all around, like Mezerich and Slonim. Rav Shmuel Berenbaum (current Mirrer Rosh HaYeshiva in Brooklyn, NY) is from Kineshin, Rav Shmuel Brudny, *zt'l,* was from Smargon and Rav Nechamtchik was from Rebzewitz. Others came from Kobrin, Lechevitch, Neswitz, Minsk, Slobodka...from all over.

In Mir I had little to do, so I helped my mother do the laundry, I swept and helped to clean the house, and I read books. I didn't go to school because I was already older, but my sister had a private teacher. In Mir we rented a house, we didn't own our own house, that was only in Kelm.

The gentiles lived outside the town and would come into town to buy what they needed, but they weren't good. They were anti-Semitic, and we were afraid of them. They came into town to drink and went out on the streets drunk. The police were very strict. Many times they would put them in jail over night or until they sobered up. But in general, everybody used to be afraid of the policemen. One of them, Avatski, used to see that the streets were kept clean. There were no sidewalks, just plain dirt, but you had to sweep the dirt in front of the house and keep it clean. If you didn't, you got a summons. When I fed my children outside I would tell them that Avatski is coming and that they should eat everything all up. Even today I am afraid of a policeman, because what you're born with stays with you. They didn't treat the Jews well. Any little thing and they used to come and hit...they would come and give you a good hit. In Poland they were bad, in Germany the police were good, that's the irony of it. In Germany they left you alone. Jews had rights and they were enforced. Many of the German judges were Jews. But really no one is good to the *Yidden*, they always hate us.

When I first came to Mir, Rav Lazer Yudel (Rabbi Eliezer Yehuda Finkel) was the Rosh HaYeshiva and Rav Yeruchem (Levovitz) was the *Mashgiach*. Rabbi Avrohom Hirsch Kamai was the Rov of Mir, and he also said a *shiur* in the yeshiva.

The gentiles lived outside the town and would come into town to buy what they needed, but they weren't good. They were anti-Semitic, and we were afraid of them.

Talmidim in the Mirrer Yeshiva's Beis Medrash, c.1932

Ben Zion Foxman Collection, Agudath Israel Archives, NY

My father suffered with stomach problems, so my mother put challah away for him for the whole week. Once a poor man came and said that he can't eat bread, only challah. My father took the challah he needed for the week and gave it to him.

My father had no official position, he learned, and the American *bochurim* would come to the house to speak with him in learning. Because of this we didn't have any real income. We used to borrow money and pay back, borrow and pay back. My father used to get a little bit of *chalukah*. It was very hard.

I want to tell you a story about my father. His father was *nifter* at 70 years of age, but before he died he told my father to take care of his stepmother as if she were his real mother. So even though we had almost nothing, he would send her money every week. To be an *almonah* then was a very, very difficult thing. People used to go through the streets and yell, 'give a piece of wood for the *almonah*, give a piece of bread for the *almonah*...' that's how they helped an *almonah* survive.

When we were in Kletzk my father had no problem because he had *a parnosah*, but when we went to the Mir and had no *parnosah*...he didn't tell my mother, but he sent the same amount anyway. He used to borrow money for the family and his stepmother, and I would go to the post office and mail it out to her. Because he had no income, my mother would tell him that he was a *glazer*, a glass worker, because he "took the glass pane from one window and then put it in the other." He borrowed money from the American *bochurim*, but when he went to Petach Tikvah and had a salaried position he paid the money back. Some of the Americans gave him the money as a present.

There were many, many poor people in the cities who went from house to house collecting, trying to get a couple of pennies. They used to come from other cities as well, not only from Mir. They knocked on the door and ask to receive a *nedovah*, sometimes they asked for food. You gave the poor whatever you had in the house. My father suffered with stomach problems, so my mother put challah away for him for the whole week. Once a poor man came and said that he can't eat bread, only challah. My father took the challah he needed for the week and gave it to him. My mother told him that "if the man doesn't get challah by you, he is going to get challah by someone else, but for you I can't go out and beg! So what are you going to have for yourself?" He answered her that the Sages taught that a poor person who is used to eating fat duck meat must be given such food to eat. A *talmid* with torn shoes once came to the house to talk with my father. My father had two pairs of shoes, one for Shabbos and one for the weekdays. He asked the *bochur* what size shoe he wears, went to his room, took his Shabbos shoes and gave them to the *bochur*. Shoes were expensive in those days, but he just gave them to the student.

Partial view of a street in the town of Mir, Poland, c.1932

Rebbetzin Zlota Ginsburg Collection

Talmidim from the Mirrer Yeshiva in Poland, 1938

That's how it was in Europe then, we were all very poor. The Rosh Yeshiva, Rabbi Lazer Yudel, sent us some money before Rosh Hashanah every year.

My sister was 13 then. She had a *rebbe* and she also learned a little Hebrew and

Shlomie Abraham

Mirrer Yeshiva as it appears today in Byelarus—used as a Post Office

English. When the girls were 17 or 18 they didn't go to school anymore, and since no one had any money to buy things, we used to buy geese from the market, pluck the feathers, buy some material and make our own feather pillows for when we would be married.

My wedding took place on a Tuesday, and my parents left the next Sunday for Petach Tikvah because they had certificates to enter Palestine. At that time the British wouldn't let you enter Eretz Yisrael without formal permission. There was a yeshiva in Petach Tikvah, and the Rosh Yeshiva, Rav Reuven Katz sent tickets for my parents to come. He knew that my father was *Mashgiach* in Kletzk, and he also knew about him from the Mir...that he was a popular person. My parents stayed in Petach Tikvah for about three years until Rav Yeruchem was *nifter,* then they returned to Mir and my father became the *Mashgiach*. That was in 1938, a year before the war.

I was twenty-one and a half when I was married. I knew who my husband was because I knew the *bochurim* in the yeshiva. They would come to the house to talk to my father, so I knew him from the house. My husband came to the Mir at 16 when my father was the temporary *Mashgiach* before Rav Yeruchem came back from Lita. My father liked my husband very much, and thought when I'm ready to marry if this *bochur* was still available he would like to take him as a son-in-law. When I was ready for marriage my husband was still a *bochur* (he was 8 years older, I was 21 and he was 29), my father asked Rav Yeruchem to present the *shidduch* to my husband. It was a first *shidduch* for both of us. We met in the house and sat and talked for a few hours. In Europe you didn't go out on a date. He came to the house about seven times. We sat in the dining room, we didn't have a kitchen, just a small area for cooking. Rich people had a kitchen that they called a salon, but the poor only had a small dining room.

I'll tell you something interesting. When we first started to meet, I taught in a Bais Yaakov school in the afternoon. The girls who went to public school in the morning had *Limudei Kodesh* studies in the afternoon, and I taught one of the classes. The house where my husband rented a room was three houses away from were I taught.

The afternoon of our first meeting it was raining, and I was holding my umbrella while going to teach. Meanwhile, my husband was coming home from the yeshiva to change before coming to the house that evening. As we passed each other our umbrellas became tangled, leaving us standing together under the umbrellas. I was so embarrassed to be standing there, stuck like that. We didn't see each other coming and now here we were standing together under the umbrellas. When I finished teaching I ran home and told my father what happened. After *Ma'ariv* my father told Rav Yeruchem

We met in the house and sat and talked for a few hours. In Europe you didn't go out on a date. He came to the house about seven times. (and) we sat in the dining room.

A girls' cheder in Laskarzew, Poland

what took place. Rav Yeruchem told him that it was a sign that "they'll stand together under the *chuppah*."

My father was a *talmid* of Rav Yeruchem. Rav Yeruchem was the *Mashgiach* in Radin when my father learned there, and was the one who sent my father to Kelm.

Anyway...we met seven times, but my husband was concerned that since we had no money it might not be the best time to marry. He was worried how we were going to support ourselves. My father didn't push us. He didn't believe in that—if you want the *shidduch*, good, and if you don't want the *shidduch,* also good. That's how he felt. He wasn't like some people who go looking for the best, he felt that this was what was good for me. There wasn't much for me to discuss about the evenings we met with my father because he knew the *bochur* so well.

My husband was from Lida, a little *shtot* near Vilna. Poland isn't like America, it's not so big, maybe a little bigger than New York State. There were about 3 million *Yidden* in Poland before the war. We made a *kiyum* (commitment to marry) in the house. We prepared one table for the men, and another one for the ladies, with cakes and cookies. My father already had his tickets to Eretz Yisroel for 6 weeks hence, so my *tenaim* was on the 5th of *Tammuz,* and my *chasanah* was on the 15th of *Av*. Right after the *tenaim* my husband went to his father and stepmother to have clothes made for himself.

Our *chasanah* I described to you before. There were two houses, that of the

Rebbetzin Zlota Ginsburg Collection

*Rabbi Ephraim Mordechai Ginsburg
Rosh HaYeshiva of Mirrer Yeshiva
in America*

Rov and that of the Rosh Yeshiva, and in between the houses was the yeshiva, the shul was one street away. The men were by the Rov's house and the ladies were by the Rosh Yeshiva's house. For the *badekin,* the men came from the Rov's house to the Rosh Yeshiva's house. After the *badekin,* we went to the *chuppah* which was set up by the side of the shul. When the marriage ceremony was finished everyone went back to the Rosh Yeshiva's house for the *seuda* (meal). The men were in one room and the women were in another room. Because it was during the vacation most of the *bochurim* were away, so there weren't too many guests.

We paid a lady to prepare the meal. But it wasn't like it is today. First we had soup and then chopped liver. For the main course we had a loaf made from chopped meat with eggs in the middle. With the meat we served farfel and we had

My father was a talmid of Rav Yeruchem. Rav Yeruchem was the Mashgiach in Radin when my father learned there, and was the one who sent my father to Kelm.

Shlomie Abraham

Radin Yeshiva as it appears today in Byelarus—used as a social hall

Rebbetzin Zlota Ginsburg Collection

Rebbetzin Zlota Ginsburg together with her oldest child and sister (behind the bench) in Keidan

> *My father spoke at our (chasunah). He emphasized that A choson should know that he has taken upon himself a tremendous obligation to love his wife like himself, and to honor her more than himself. A man's obligation to his wife is very, very great.*

summer. The Rosh HaYeshiva went to Germany for a rest at the health spas and baths that were popular with the Torah leaders in the summer. The yeshiva wasn't closed, but there were no *shiurim,* so many of the *bochurim* went home. The *talmidim* who stayed during the summer to learn continued to receive their stipends from the yeshiva. Everybody came back for the *Elul zeman.*

It was the custom in Europe that the *rabbonim* spoke during the *seudah.* My father spoke at ours. He emphasized two main points. The first was *"b'mah zocheh b'shem tov,"* how important it is to earn a good reputation. And then he told my husband that he shouldn't think once a man is married everything is settled and all is good. Not quite. A *choson* should know that he has taken upon himself a tremendous obligation to love his wife like himself, and to honor her more than himself. A man's obligation to his wife is very, very great. The son of the *Mashgiach* from Kobrin spoke as well... A lot of our guests were killed during the war...

We lived in Mir after the *chasunah* and rented rooms in a private house. There were three bedrooms, a dining room and a kitchen. One bedroom was for my landlady, my sister had another and my husband and I had the third. It was crowded in the house, but I didn't have children for three and a half years, and by then my father was back in Mir as the *Mashgiach* after Rav Yeruchem passed away.[29]

compote for dessert. That's all, a regular meal. There were one or two people playing music, but they only played as we walked to the *chuppah.*

I was escorted to the *chuppah* by Rebbetzin Brudny's mother and someone else..she was later killed by Hitler. My parents walked behind us. My husband was escorted by Rebbitzin Brudny's father, and Rabbi Avrohom Kaplinsky, who learned in the Mir. I don't remember who was the *mesader kiddushin.* The Rov and the Rosh HaYeshiva weren't there since it was in the

After the wedding my sister stayed with me for a couple of years. She had something like polio in one leg, so my husband took her to Warsaw for medical treatment. Since she couldn't walk well on that leg, they wanted her to use a certain type of shoe that would help her. This embar-

29. One of Reb Yeruchem's sons, his son's wife and two children were killed by Hitler. Rebbetzin Levovitz and her other three sons and a daughter escaped to Japan, and then to America. The Rebbetzin was *nifter* in the United states in 1948.

rassed her, and she didn't want to come back to Mir like that, so she remained in Warsaw at my step-grandmother's house. Soon after, my father sent her a certificate to enter Palestine, so she went to Eretz Yisrael.

Ruchoma Shain was in Mir when I was married. She left just before the war. All the Americans left then, because the American Consulate warned them to leave. Some left earlier and some later. They went by boat, there was very little air flight then. When Ruchoma came to Mir after her marriage, she brought her wedding dress with her for other girls to use. It was her gown I wore for my wedding picture.

My first child was 8 months old when the war broke out. In Shanghai I had three boys, and then in America I had another girl and two more boys. After we left Mir with the yeshiva at the beginning of World War II, we went to Vilna for approximately half a year (11/39-5/40), to Keidan for half a year (until 12/40 or 1/41), and then we left for Japan."

World War II: *The Miracle of the Mir*

"The war started September 1, 1939, right before Rosh Hashanah. Immediately after Succos we heard the Russians were planning to enter Poland. All the *shtetlach* on Poland's eastern border were being occupied by the Russians, but

Ruchoma Shain (2nd from top) with Yocheved Levenstein (top), Zlota Levenstein (Ginsburg), on the bottom left and Liba Gulevsky to her right

German soldiers removing a border barrier during the invasion of Poland, September 1939

In Europe they were not strict about using butter made by a gentile, because butter can only be made from kosher milk.

Vilna was a free city.[30] Since it was free, and the Russians hadn't entered, the Mir planned to go there, as did many other yeshivas. When the yeshiva left for Vilna my father remained behind, he wasn't so worried about the Russians. He decided that if any of the *talmidim* would remain in Mir, he would remain with those who stayed behind. So he and my mother stayed while my husband and I went to Vilna with my sister. My father didn't want the young people to stay because he was worried that the communists wouldn't let them marry properly. For a young girl it wasn't good to remain, so he sent my sister with us. We went to Vilna by train.

In the end my parents didn't stay very long either, because the whole yeshiva evacuated to Vilna. When he saw that everyone left, and then received a telegram from my husband urging that he come right away, he and my mother left

Yeshiva bochurim and other Jewish refugees upon their arrival in the port city of Tsuruga, Japan

and came to Vilna. But it wasn't safe for the yeshiva to stay in Vilna for too long since the Lithuanian officials were pressuring them to leave. At that point the yeshiva moved to Keidan, and when it was no longer safe in Keidan the yeshiva divided up and went to four different towns: Krak, Krakinova, Shat and Ramigolah. My father walked from one village to the other to be *m'chazek* the *talmidim* and to give a *shmues*. My husband and I remained in Vilna with my sister because the Brisker Rov was in Vilna and my husband wanted to attend his *shiurim*.

In Europe they were not strict about using butter made by a gentile, because butter can only be made from kosher milk. However, the Brisker Rov was strict not to use any butter unless it was made by a Jew. I used to make the butter for the Brisker Rov while we were in Vilna, and his sons, Reb Yosef Ber and Reb Dovid would come and pick it up.[31]

There was a large influx of Jews and yeshivas from all over Poland and Lithuania into Vilna. Because of this it was very difficult to find a place to stay. We had only one room and a little place for my sister, but then she went with my parents so it was only my husband, the baby and me. My parents lived in Keidan. Life in Lithuania itself wasn't so hard. There was enough food for the refugees in Vilna and the surrounding areas. We had bread, chicken, eggs and even meat for Shabbos, and a little stove in our room to keep us warm. Of the many people who came to Vilna, some had relatives in America who arranged for them to come to the United

---

30. See section on The History of Vilna.

31. Rabbi Eliezer Ginsburg, Rosh Kollel of the Mir Yeshiva in Brooklyn, NY, adds the following story about his mother during her stay in Vilna: "The Brisker Rov gave shiur at night. My parents lived in a small room off a courtyard and the owner of the courtyard would lock the gate early every evening, but my father wouldn't come home until midnight. My mother would wait by the gate each night and unlock it for my father, even in the freezing cold of the winter. This is how much she loved his learning."

States. It was difficult, it was a *shlep*, but they went (in the end it saved their lives, but we didn't know this at the time).

In Kovno there was a Japanese Consulate issuing transit visas to go through Japan, but you needed a final destination. Our place of final destination was the island of Curacao. We were able to obtain transit visas and left with the yeshiva by train, through Russia, to the Port of Vladivostok. The yeshiva landed in the Japanese port of Tsuruga and settled in the harbor city of Kobe.

Almost the entire yeshiva left intact, but some did not go because of the cost, they also thought that the Russians would never allow such a thing...that it would be a waste. Those who remained behind were killed. My husband said no matter what the cost, if the yeshiva is going, we are going. My father also said we should go.

A man from the yeshiva, Rabbi Zupnick, went to the American Consulate for all of us because he knew English. The transit visas cost 180 American dollars! Where were we going to get that much money in the middle of Europe during a war? But that's how much the Russians wanted. Rabbi Avrohom Kalmanowitz, the Mirrer Rosh Yeshiva in America, raised the money through the Vaad Hatzala and sent it to us in Vilna. Some people had relatives in America who sent them money. The only people who didn't have the option to go were those without a passport, otherwise Rabbi Kalmanowitz raised enough money for everyone. Not only the Mirrer *talmidim* went, many of Rav Aharon Kotler's *talmidim* from Kletzk went as well.[32]

Before leaving for Japan we prepared salami for supper and dry American cheese for lunch and breakfast. Tea we were able to get on the train, and fresh bread my husband would buy whenever the train stopped. We slept in a little berth; there were four in our compartment, one on top of the other. The baby and I slept in the bottom one, my husband slept in the next one, and two *bochurim* slept in the ones on top. We spent Shabbos on the train. We ate in the compartments where we slept...the same thing...cheese for breakfast and lunch, and salami for dinner. There were two or three small toilets on the train, you could wash your hands and face, but you couldn't shower.

My father and the Rosh HaYeshiva, Rabbi Chaim Shmulevitz, did not give any *shiurim* on the train. You see, everyone was afraid because we thought someone was coming to catch us doing something wrong. Since it was a time of war and many people had false papers, the conductors made frequent document checks.

Rabbi Chaim Shmulevitz
The Mirrer Rosh HaYeshiva, *who along with Reb Chatzkel, escaped and led the yeshiva to Shanghai*

My father and the Rosh HaYeshiva, Rabbi Chaim Shmulevitz, did not give any shiurim *on the train. You see, everyone was afraid because we thought someone was coming to catch us doing something wrong.*

---

32. The student is referred to the book: Bunim, Amos, **A FIRE IN HIS SOUL,** (Feldheim, NY, 1989) for an exhaustive and authoritative accounting of the inspirational and vital work of the Vaad Hatzala.

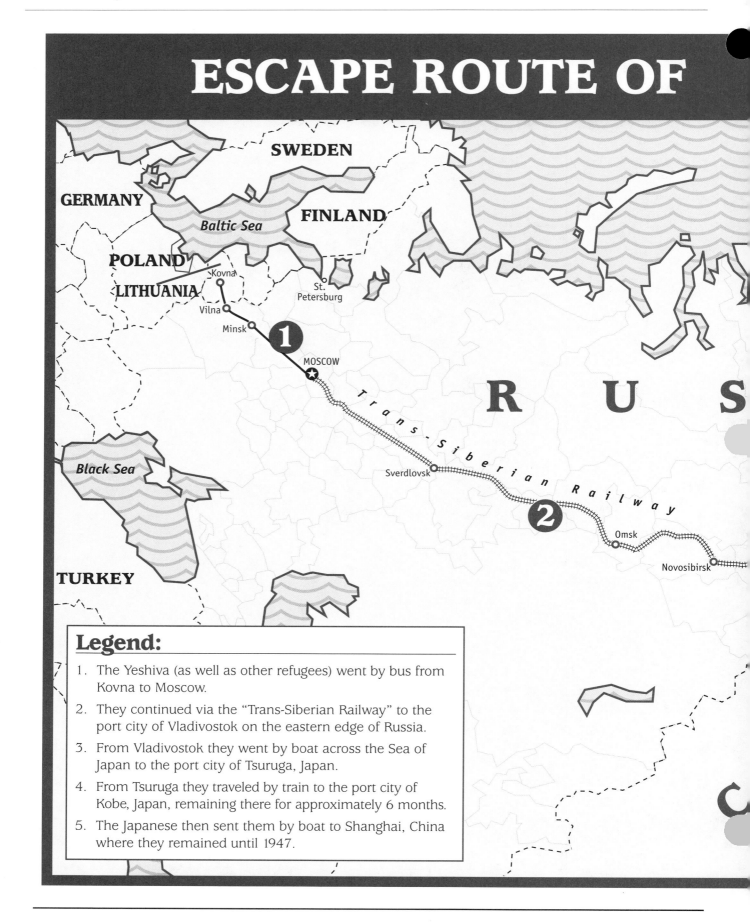

ESCAPE ROUTE OF

Legend:

1. The Yeshiva (as well as other refugees) went by bus from Kovna to Moscow.

2. They continued via the "Trans-Siberian Railway" to the port city of Vladivostok on the eastern edge of Russia.

3. From Vladivostok they went by boat across the Sea of Japan to the port city of Tsuruga, Japan.

4. From Tsuruga they traveled by train to the port city of Kobe, Japan, remaining there for approximately 6 months.

5. The Japanese then sent them by boat to Shanghai, China where they remained until 1947.

THE MIRRER YESHIVA

Sea of Okhotsk

S I A

Krasnoyarsk

Irkutsk

Birobidzhan

Khabarovsk

C H I N A

Vladivostok

Sea of Japan

3

JAPAN

Tsuruga

4

Kobe

KOREA

Yellow Sea

5

Shanghai

East China Sea

Reb Chatzkel Levenstein officiating at a chasunah in Shanghai

We landed in the port city of Tsuruga, and then went overland through the city of Nagoya to Kobe. There were about 25 Jewish families living in Kobe, and some of them were financially well-off. They knew that the refugees were coming and they came to be *m'kabol panim.* They had already arranged our rooms and food. We arrived in the middle of the winter, and remained for approximately half a year, until it was fairly well known that there would be a war between America and Japan. Then the Japanese sent the yeshiva to Shanghai. We didn't need special visas since everyone was sent at once. The Japanese were good to us...it was *min hashomayim,* a miracle from Heaven, that they should treat us as they did.

The Japanese worshiped idols. The country is beautiful and it was like springtime all year round. There are many high mountains where they placed the idols, and every morning they brought them food and water. They are a very organized people. Each morning at 8:00am they exercised— everyone, even the children.

Everyone was sitting and learning, hoping that they wouldn't be caught. *Boruch Hashem*, no one was caught, no one was discovered.

After three weeks we came to the Russian port city of Vladivostok (located on the southeastern most tip of the USSR, close to the northeastern most tip of Korea, and right on the Sea of Japan) and left by ship for Japan. We were on a ship with animals and had no roof over our heads. Everyone was crowded together and there was no toilet—you had to go to the side of the boat. It was terrible, and this is how we traveled for thirty-six hours.

There were about 25 Jewish families living in Kobe, and some of them were financially well off. They knew that the refugees were coming and they came to be m'kabol panim. They had already arranged our rooms and food.

Title page from an edition of a Gemora printed in Shanghai, 1943

There were no showers or toilets in the houses, so they bathed together outdoors, everyone together—men, women and children. Nonetheless they treated us reasonably well. We had rice and bread to eat, but no wine for *kiddush*, and there wasn't much fish because most of it was *treif* (not kosher). We didn't starve, however, and there were about 500 of us in the yeshiva's group. It was an open miracle that we survived the war as we did.

The Mirrer Yeshiva learning in the 'Beis Aharon' synagogue in Shanghai, China. First row, far left is Reb Chatzkel, second from right is Reb Chaim Shmulevitz

The facade of 'Beis Aharon' synagogue which was located on Museum Road

My father and Reb Chaim organized the affairs of the yeshiva. They had a very good relationship. We had a *Beis Medrash* in Kobe, and also in Shanghai. The whole escape, and the fact that we had two places for the yeshiva to go and learn in safety...miracles, all miracles. In Kobe, the *Beis Hamedrash* was already set up, and some of the yeshiva people brought a few *seforim* (books) of their own. Rabbi Avraham Kalmanowitz sent *gemoras* from America.

People were busy trying to arrange visas and travel documents with the American Consulate in Shanghai. They were writing to relatives in America to send them the necessary papers so they could im-

DAY OF MOURNING AND PRAYER

IN COMMEMORATION OF THE JEWISH VICTIMS OF NAZI TERROR

Jewish brothers and sisters in Shanghai!

The greatest part of European Jewry has been exterminated; more than six million of our best and dearest have met the death of martyrs. In Nazi camps, they were tortured, murdered, burnt, gassed, subjected to the most horrible sufferings...

Millions of defenceless Jewish women were tortured to death; infants were snatched from their mothers' breast and cast into fire, before the eyes of their helpless parents.

These holy martyrs have not found even a Jewish grave. Nothing has remained of them, but heaps of ashes at Maidanek, Oswiencim, Treblinka....

Ancient centers of glorious Jewish Life and Culture were changed into ruins. Thousand-year-old communities were destroyed. Their members buried alive in mass graves.

Our Houses of Worship were burnt down, our Torah—Scrolls torn to pieces, our cultural and spiritual treasures destroyed

Standing before the greatest destruction of our people, wrapped in mourning, beaten and faint, the holy souls of our near and dear brothers and sisters hover before our eyes and appeal to us to acknowledge the whole burden of this terrific tragedy, calling to us to unite around our remaining cultural Treasures and our Tradition which will give us the possibility for our renaissance.

Thursday, the 27th of Adar (February 28th, 1946) has been set aside as a Day of Yiskor, of mourning and prayer to honour the memory of our dearones who gave their lives because they were Jews. A half—day fast (until 1 p. m.) has been declared for that day, to be observed by all adults, with the exception of sick and weak persons.

Furthermore, all Jews are being requested to keep their stores and Offices closed up to 1 p. m., and to abstain from all manner of work, so as to be able to participate in large numbers in the Yiskor service to be held in the New Synagogue (102 Rte Tenant de la Tour) where prayers and speeches will be rendered to demonstrate our solidarity and sympathy with the great grief of the Jewish people.

The service will begin at 10 a. m sharp.

We appeal to the whole Jewish Community, who with God's assistance, has been spared from the tragic fate of other Jewish congregations, to prove that it is conscious of its miraculous deliverance, and to repay for our saved lives by enabling the remaining Jewish children in Europe to live.

Let every one of us contribute a day's livelihood for the deliverance of remaining Jewish orphans, still confined to camps kept in Gentile hands, so as to redeem and find them a new home in Eretz Israel, to be raised in the spirit of our holy Thora, to be free and upright people!

No Jew can abstain himself from participating in this tribute to the martyrs of our nation. Let us all unite in prayer and in hope for a better future. Let us all unite for the redemption of the Jewish Youth in Europe!

Shanghai Ashkenazi Jewish Communal Association

Shanghai Sephardic Jewish Community

Juedische Gemeinde

Rabbi M. Ashkenazi

Rabbi Kalish (Amshener)

Rabbi Levenstein
(Mashgiach of Mirror Jeshivah)

Rabbi Shmulevich
(Dean of Mirror Jeshivah)

*A 'Day of Yizkor,'
Feb. 28, 1946 established by the
leaders of the Shanghai community to honor
the memory of the Six Million 'Kedoshim' of the Holocaust*

*Rabbi Chaim Shmulevitz
in his younger years*

migrate, and some were able to leave. Rabbi Aharon Kotler came to America, where he joined Rabbi Kalmanowitz, Rabbi Eliezer Silver and lay leaders like Irving Bunim, Mike Tress and Stephen Klein to spearhead and guide the *Hatzala* movement in its attempt to save as many Jews as possible from Europe. My husband received a certificate from the Brisker Rov, because he learned with him in Vilna, but he didn't want to leave my

father and mother, or my sister. My parents were older and my father didn't have a certificate to leave, and even if he had he wouldn't have left the yeshiva. Rav Chaim (Shmulevitz) also didn't want to leave, so they were together in Shanghai for six years.

The trip from Kobe to Shanghai took a week. I'm telling you Hashem gives strength "*hanosen la'yoef koach*," (...Who gives strength to the weary). You can't imagine what it was like, all of this turmoil and running and not knowing what would be the next day. The Poles, Lithuanians, Russians...they all hate us. If we didn't clearly know how they felt about us then, we certainly know now. At first I depended upon my husband for everything, so I didn't think so much about what I was going through. I was only 24, I was young. My mother was very upset. She was an elderly lady and said of her *avos avoseinu* (her father's fathers) that they didn't bring her into the world to live among such people as the Chinese, that she never saw such a people in her entire life. The Japanese were much more refined than the Chinese...they worshiped idols, but they were more refined. One can't imagine the turmoil unless he's in the situation. My parents and sister lived in the same room with my husband and me and the children. We divided the room with a curtain, and there was a little stove with which to heat and cook. In the summer it was very hot, 100 degrees and higher.

Once, on a very hot day, the *bochurim* went to swim and cool off, but my father remained learning at his *shtender*, only pausing to shake the edge of his sleeve a bit to cool off his arm. He was fully dressed, long coat and all. That's how he was. You can't imagine what we lived through, how we struggled, but we weren't afraid, *and* we remained alive! When we came to America we weren't youngsters anymore… the youngest was Rav Shmuel Berenbaum (the present Mirrer Rosh Yeshiva, Brooklyn, NY) and his *chaverim.*

Everyone was close in Shanghai. It was a time of war, and in such a time people see how much they really need each other. There were other refugees there as well, including about 20,000 German refugees that ran away from Hitler. Most were Jews, but there were some non-Jews as well.

Conclusion

When you're young you don't think so much about what you go through, but it leaves an impression on your nerves. When times are bad Hashem gives you extra strength to carry on…a special strength. Just like a person receives a *neshamah yiseirah* (an additional soul) for Shabbos to enjoy the spiritual and physical blessings of the Shabbos, so does Hashem give extra strength in times of trouble. I felt this all the time after I lost my husband. We came to America in 1947, and my husband was *nifter* in 1960. I had 7 children (one son was *nifter* in 1952), and we had no *parnosah,* but I didn't have, *chas vashalom,* any complaints to Hashem or think that it was too hard. No. I feel that Hashem gives special strength in each situation…"

Agudath Israel Archives, NY

The building in Shanghai which housed the talmidim of the Mirrer Yeshiva

Rebbetzin Zlota Ginsburg Collection

The Bais Yaakov Girls' School in Shanghai established by the refugees

MIRRER YESHIVA IN ERETZ YISRAEL, 5756/1996

Rabbi Nosson Tzvi Finkel, Shlita— Rosh HaYeshiva

Rabbi Rafael Shmulevitz, Shlita— Rosh HaYeshiva

The Yeshiva Building which houses the Beis Hamedrash, Dining Room and Dormitory

The Yeshiva's Beis Hamedrash

MIRRER YESHIVA IN AMERICA, 5756/1996

Zev Saftlas

Rabbi Shmuel Berenbaum, Shlita— Rosh HaYeshiva

Zev Saftlas

Rabbi Shraga Moshe Kalmanowitz, Shlita— Rosh HaYeshiva

The Yeshiva Building which houses the Beis Hamedrash, High School, Dining Room, and Dormitory. The attached building on the far right houses the Mirrer Yeshiva Ketana, the elementary school

Zev Saftlas

The Yeshiva's Beis Hamedrash

PORTRAIT OF A LITHUANIAN TORAH PERSONALITY:

Vignettes of the Ohr Yechezkel, Rabbi Yechezkel Levenstein, ZT"L

In the Kelm Talmud Torah there was a fixed time for the study of *mussar,* for one full hour before the time of the evening prayers. One of the *talmidim* who learned in the yeshiva with the *Mashgiach* related that the *Ohr Yechezkel* learned *mussar* with the same diligence, desire and strength through the entire hour without pause. However, it was not just during the *Mussar seder* (period) that one could see the *Ohr Yechezkel* learn with such total involvement. To see him *daven* (pray) was to see a servant standing in humility before his Master, a soul dressed in the garment of his body, yet completely detached from the physical world. He was the picture of a man in full realization of his purpose in this world, who was running to fulfill this purpose with all of his might. He was unrelenting in his battle with the *yetzer hara* (evil inclination), never taking his mind off his foe or retiring from the battle.

Reb Chatzkel in his younger years

It is well known that the *Ohr Yechezkel* did not sleep during the day, not during the week and not on Shabbos. He considered such relaxation an interruption of his *Avodas Hashem*, of his day long service of learning and prayer.

The *Ohr Yechezkel* related that in 1935, when he moved to Eretz Yisrael to assume the position of *mashgiach* in the yeshiva in Petach Tikvah, he was asked by the Mirrer *mashgiach*, Rabbi Yeruchem Levovitz, what he found lacking in the Mir that caused him to make such a move. Reb Yechezkel answered that his whole life he toiled to gain greater levels of *emunah* (belief in Hashem), to reach the level that his belief in Hashem's Presence should reside firmly in his heart and mind, yet he found that he had still not attained his goal. He felt by moving to Eretz Yisrael, the land of the *Avos*, the place where G-d's Presence is revealed on earth, that perhaps there he would merit to attain perfect *emunah,* his great desire.

Rebbetzin Zlota Ginsburg Collection

Ceremony at the City Hall of San Francisco in 1947 welcoming the refugees arriving from Shanghai, China. Reb Chatzkel is in the center of the front row.

The present Rosh Yeshiva of the Ponevezh Yeshiva, *Moreinu Rabbeinu* Rabbi Menachem M. Shach, *Shlita,* related that while a *talmid* in the Kletzk Yeshiva when the *Ohr Yechezkel* was *mashgiach*, Reb Yechezkel would come to him and tell him to learn with this *talmid*, to help out that *talmid*, to try to give *chizuk* (comfort and support) to yet another *talmid*. The *Mashgiach* was aware of the needs of each and every *talmid* constantly, there was nothing hidden from him. The *Mashgiach* once confided in someone that while in Kletzk he never left the *Beis Hamedrash* (study hall) early because he knew that a certain student would leave before the official end of the study period if the *Mashgiach* was not there. In order to prevent this, Reb Yechezkel never left early. This was in addition to his belief that as *Mashgiach* of the yeshiva it was his responsibility to remain to supervise the *talmidim* throughout all of the study periods.

In 1957, when the *Mashgiach* was in Ponevezh Yeshiva in B'nei Brak, his son-in-law, Rav Ephriam Mordechai Ginsburg, *zt"l,* (one of the *roshei yeshiva* of the Mir Yeshiva in Brooklyn, NY) invited him to his daughter's wedding in the United States. Not only was this Rabbi Ginsburg's oldest child, but it was also the *Mashgiach's* first grandchild. In addition, Rabbi Ginsburg wanted his revered father-in-law to come so that he could strengthen his ties with, and give *chizuk* and comfort to the hundreds of his *talmidim* now living in the U.S., *talmidim* who had been together with the *Mashgiach* for so many years and through so many hardships in Mir, Vilna, Russia, Japan and Shanghai. Nonetheless, the *Mashgiach* refused the invitation, explaining that he could not leave the 350 *talmidim* of the Ponevezh Yeshiva at the beginning of the new *zeman* (semester of study), knowing that a successful start to the *zeman* could mean the difference between success or failure in learning for many of the students. The *Mashgiach* later revealed that his main reason for not attending the wedding and subsequent reunion was his great feeling of responsibility to the yeshiva. A yeshiva requires constant and persistent supervision, and Heaven forbid, that he should abandon this responsibility even for the least amount of time.

The *Mashgiach* once recounted that the years spent with the Mir Yeshiva in Shanghai (though it was a time of great physical deprivation) were years of success. "Shanghai was a time of success...five years of success...of toil in learning, of toil in *davening* (prayer), of toil in *mussar*...five years of success."

The *Mashgiach* felt and expressed his sense of eternal gratitude to the Creator for the extraordinary merit to remain with the yeshiva during this great and awesome

Rosh Yeshiva of the Ponevezh Yeshiva, Moreinu Rabbeinu Rabbi Elazor Menachem M. Shach, *Shlita, with Rabbi Eliezer Ginsburg, Reb Chatzkel's grandson*

time, and the opportunity to be *m'chazek* (spiritually uplift and strengthen) the *talmidim* while caring for them as both their mother and father.

The *Mashgiach* was quick to teach the importance of working on behalf of the *k'lal* (congregation). In one of his letters to a contemporary Torah scholar and educator, the *Mashgiach* expressed his great delight that this personality decided to return to his teaching post at one of the great yeshivos. The *Mashgiach* stated that "...great is the merit to teach the many, so great is this responsibility that one must overlook one's own needs in order to serve the needs of the congregation, because from the great yeshivos that teach Torah and *yiras Shomayim* (fear of Heaven)...from this is the purpose of creation fulfilled."

After the Mir found refuge in Shanghai, the *talmidim* expressed the desire to learn one of the *Masechtos* in *Seder Kodshim* (The Order of Sacrifices). The *Mashgiach*

The Mashgiach *once recounted... (though it was a time of great physical deprivation) "Shanghai was a time of success... five years of success...of toil in learning, of toil in davening (prayer), of toil in mussar... five years of success."*

The Mashgiach *felt and expressed his sense of eternal gratitude to the Creator for the extraordinary merit to remain with the yeshiva during this great and awesome time.*

refused their request. He told the *talmidim* that after the war the Jewish people would need to be rebuilt, and that they would need Torah leaders familiar with the more practical laws of everyday life: Shabbos and *Yom Tov,* marriage, prayer, business and kashrus. The *talmidim* couldn't understand his words. What world? What would be left from the utter destruction they were witness to and saved from? The *Mashgiach* remained firm in his resolve: "At such a time we must be prepared to build a new generation, to rebuild what has been destroyed and to replant the song of Torah within the hearts of the next generation. LEARN! REVIEW! Create new *chiddushei Torah* (new and novel interpretations of the *Gemoras*)! You will see that the new generation will be waiting for you, and through you will Torah again be returned to its splendor."

The *Mashgiach* would constantly teach the necessity to toil in Torah and *yiras Shomayim* (fear of Heaven). He would stress that without toil and constant effort one cannot expect to attain the lofty goals that are expected of him in this world. In his letters he quoted the saying of the Sages from the *Gemora Berachos* that Hashem gave three *matonos tovos* (good presents) to the Jewish people that can be attained only through hardship: Torah, Eretz Yisrael and *Olam Haba* (the World to Come). "We see from this," he would state, "that without great effort and toil a person cannot attain any meaningful achievement or spiritual elevation. How foolish, therefore, are the people who think that without such effort and dedication they can attain these three treasures, whose goodness benefits one in both this world and in the World to Come." The *Mashgiach* would regularly emphasize this teaching by quoting the words of Rabbeinu Yona in *Shaarei Teshuva,* "What hope can a *nivrah* (a created be-

Yeshivas Ponevezh in Bnei Brak

The majestic Aron HaKodesh in the Yeshiva's Beis HaMedrash

ing) have if he fails to direct the endeavors and efforts of his soul's yearning in the fulfillment of those things for which he was created!"

The *Mashgiach* would often urge the *talmidim* to consider the exalted nature of prayer. He would repeat the saying of the Sages (*Gemora Berachos*) that "prayer is one of the things that stands at the very highest heights of Heaven, yet is disregarded by man. "That," according to the *Chovos Halevovos*, "prayer without proper intent is like the body without a soul." The

He would stress that without toil and constant effort one cannot expect to attain the lofty goals that are expected of him in this world.

It was a popular practice for people to come from all over Eretz Yisrael to Reb Chatzkel's Purim Seudah in Ponevezh for a brachah. Rabbi Chaim Ginsburg, Reb Chatzkel's grandson is seated to his right.

The Mashgiach would often urge the talmidim to consider the exalted nature of prayer. He would repeat the saying of the Sages (Gemora Berachos) that "prayer is one of the things that stands at the very highest heights of Heaven, yet is disregarded by man.

Mashgiach would add that even being knowledgeable of the meaning of the words does not constitute proper prayer. Rather, one must stand in prayer like a slave before his master, begging and pleading that his needs be fulfilled. Also, the *Mashgiach* felt that prayer without understanding the meaning of the words is considered "dead," with no life giving sustenance at all.

Finally, the *Mashgiach* would instruct the students to approach the acquisition of proper prayer in the following manner: First, one must know the meaning of the words of the first blessing, which if not said with understanding can cause the whole prayer to be invalid. Then, one should add on one blessing at a time, until the meaning of all of the blessings are clear. One should also do this for *Pesukei D'zimrah*, and the blessings of *Shema* and *Shema* itself. Additionally, while saying the prayers he would teach that one should strengthen his *emunah* (belief) in *Hashgachas Hashem* (Hashem's complete and unmitigated rule of all phenomena and events in the universe). He would tell the students that by

following this advice they would surely succeed in the attainment of proper prayer.

The *talmidim* of the *Mashgiach* at the Ponevezh Yeshiva would wake up each day to find the *Mashgiach* already at his place of *davening* in the *Beis Hamedrash* no less than twenty-five minutes before *davening* was scheduled to begin. He would accustom himself to prepare for *davening* in the manner of the *Chassidim Reshonim* (early Sages) who would meditate an hour before *davening* to reach a state of total and pure intellectual attachment to the prayers, devoid of any attachment in the physical world. The *talmidim* related that in this manner did, "...we see with our own eyes the true expression of prayer as it was meant to be." It is said that the *Mashgiach's* prayers never went unanswered, and that the great people of the generation would ask the *Mashgiach* to pray on their behalf.

The *Mashgiach* urged the *talmidim* to train their minds to concentrate, without distraction, on one topic for a prolonged period of time. He instructed them that this was an essential quality in contemplating upon one's *Avodas Hashem*. He once related to a student that at the age of twenty he was able to commit himself in total concentration to one idea or concept for more than twenty minutes.

The *Ohr Yechezkel* taught himself to mentally visualize *Yetzias Mitzrayim*, the Splitting of the *Yam Suf*, the Receiving of the Torah on *Har Sinai* and the miracles and wonders that Hashem wrought on behalf of *K'lal Yisroel* during their travels through the desert, not as mental images, but as three dimensional testimonies of *emunah* in the Creator and His Torah. The *Mashgiach* taught that through contemplation of these phenomena that reveal Hashem's total and complete control and mastery of creation, one can attain and experience the revelation of Hashem, today, as our forefathers did so many millennia ago. He explained that the ability to re-experience these revelations through deep contemplation is a special treasure that the Creator hid within these events at the time of their occurrence. The *talmidim* of the yeshiva relate that one who merited to hear the *Mashgiach* sing the *Shir shel Yom* on Shabbos *Shira* heard in his voice the joy of *K'lal Yisrael* as they passed through the Sea.

The *Mashgiach* once disclosed that many of the life and death decisions he made while leading the Mirrer Yeshiva on its journeys during World War II were Divinely inspired, that his *rebbaim,* the son and son-in-law of The Alter of Kelm, Rabbi Simcha Zissel Ziv, would come to him in dreams and direct his course of action.

In the following incident, described by Rabbi Shlomo Brevda, the *Mashgiach* defined the great challenge facing Orthodox Jewry in our generation. "The most inspirational moment of my life," Rabbi Brevda related, "took place over 50 years ago on a Wednesday morning at the end of one of the *Mashgiach's* regularly scheduled *shmussen*. Standing in front of the *Aron Kodesh,* addressing the yeshiva, the *Mashgiach* paused and said, '*Chazal HaKedoshim* say that in the last generations before *Moshiach* the *Emes*, the Truth, will become lost.' He stopped speaking, extended his right arm in front of him, and squinted, pointing with his right index finger to some place in the far distance. He was searching for something with great urgency. Then, he asked, 'What do *Chazal* mean? There is no longer any *Emes* left in the world?! It's no longer to be found?!' He remained standing there, pointing and peering into the distance. The whole yeshiva was spellbound. The *Mash-*

giach had never done anything like this before. His outward behavior was always so normal and natural. Yet now he just stood there pointing and staring...looking...looking for the *Emes*. The tension was palpable. Finally, he broke the silence, and in a firm voice he said, 'In our times there **still** is *Emes*. So what is the difference between now and the earlier generations? The *Emes* today is buried very, very deep, and only

Reb Chatzkel delivering a mussar shmues in front of the Aron Kodesh in Ponevezh

with great toil and constant effort will you find it. Otherwise, you can live an entire lifetime and find nothing.'"

The *Mashgiach* always stressed to all who knew him the importance of understanding the eternity of the soul—that a person was not created for his situation in this world, but for that of the World to Come. "A man is here to acquire his *Olam Haba*," the *Mashgiach* would remark, "his eternal life and joy that is without end."

When the *Mashgiach,* Reb Yechezkel Levenstein was *nifter,* the world lost one of the great servants of Hashem. His righteousness and true fear of Heaven will stand eternal and shine forth before us forever.

"A man is here to acquire his Olam Haba," the Mashgiach would remark, "his eternal life and joy that is without end."

✑ GLOSSARY OF TERMS

Ahavas Torah— love for the Torah

almonah— widow

Am Hanivchar— the Chosen Nation

Amen— word recited after a blessing to show one's acceptance of the truth of that blessing

Av— the fifth Hebrew month

Av Beis Din— chief judge of the rabbinical court

avel— mourner

Avodas Hashem— Service to G-d

avos avoseinu— our father's fathers

b'mah zocheh b'shem tov— how can one earn a good reputation

b'tzar— in pain, discomfort (physical or mental)

ba'al habayis— head of a household, working man learning part-time

badekin— covering the face of the bride with her veil

bas— daughter

bas chassidim— woman of chassidic heritage

behaimos— livestock

bein hasedorim— time between morning and afternoon study sessions

Beis Medrash (Beis Hamedrash) / Battei Medrash (pl)— study hall of a yeshiva

ben Torah— Torah scholar

bentching— prayer after meals

bimah— podium upon which the Torah is placed and read in shul

bitachon— trust in G-d

bleib— stay (Yiddish)

Bnei Torah— people who follow the teachings of the Torah

bochur / bochurim(pl)— unmarried male student

brochah / brochos (pl)— blessing(s)

Boruch Hashem— thank G-d

bubby— grandmother (Yiddish)

chachom / chachomim (pl)— sage(s)

chalif— slaughtering knife

challah— special loaf of bread made for Shabbos and Yom Tov

chalukah— stipend money given to the students for their personal needs

chanukas habayis— dedication of a new house or building

chas vashalom— Heaven forbid

chassid / chassidim (pl)— follower of the Chassidic movement

chassidic— adhering to Chassidism

chasunah— wedding

chaveirim— friends

Chaye Adam— important book of religious law

Chazal— (acronym for **CH**achomeinu **Z**ichronam **L**i'vrocha) the Sages from the time of the Mishnah and Gemora

chazon / chazonim (pl)— leader of the prayer service; cantor

chazonis— cantorial style of prayer

cheder / chadorim (pl)— orthodox elementary school (usually taught in Yiddish)

cherem— excommunication, ban

Cheshvan— the eighth Hebrew month

Chevra Shas— a group that learns Gemora

chizuk— strength

chochmah— wisdom

chodesh— month

cholent— a hot dish of meat, beans and potatoes that is served on Shabbos *(Yiddish)*

Chol Hamoed— intermediate days of Succos and Passover holidays

choson— groom

chrein— horseradish *(Yiddish)*

Chumash / Chumashim (pl)— the Five Books of Moses

churban— destruction

churban Bais Hamikdash— destruction of the Holy Temple

chuppah— wedding canopy

chutzpah— rudeness, insulting behavior

daven— pray *(Yiddish)*

dayan / dayanim (pl)— judge(s)

Din Torah— judicial case based on Torah law

divrei Torah— Torah lectures (literally, words of Torah)

derech— proper way in religious life

derech eretz— good manners, respect

dryfus— a small metal tripod

Elul— the sixth Hebrew month

emunah— faith in G-d

Eretz Yisrael— the land of Israel

erev— before, eve of... (erev Pesach, erev Shabbos)

farfel kugel— a pudding made of grain *(Yiddish)*

frum— religious *(Yiddish)*

frum balabatim— religious working men who are heads of households

frumer yid— a religious Jew *(Yiddish)*

g'vir— man of great wealth

Galus— exile, Diaspora

gaon / gaonim (pl)— genius; brilliant Torah scholar

gedolim— great religious leaders

Gehinnom— purgatory

gemach— interest free loan organization

Gemora / Gemoras (pl)— book of the Talmud

get / gittin (pl)— bill of divorce

glazer— glass worker

goyim— gentiles

goyishe chasunah— gentile wedding

goyishe minhag— gentile custom

groiser mentschen— great people *(Yid.)*

groiser tzaddik— exceedingly righteous person *(Yiddish)*

hakafos— dancing with the Torah on Simchas Torah

halachah— Jewish law

Hallel— song of praise composed of the *Tehillim* written by King David

hanhaleh— administration

Hanosen la'yoef koach— "Who gives strength to the weary" (a quote from Hebrew prayer)

Hashem— G-d, the Creator (lit. "the Name")

hatzalah— rescue

Kabalah— mystical teachings of the Torah

kabolos panim— receiving of the wedding guests

kallah— bride

kashruth— laws of keeping kosher

kavod— honor

kavonah— thoughtful intent

kedushah— holiness

kiddush— prayer over wine made before eating on Sabbath and holidays

Kisay Hakoved— (Hashem's) holy throne

kittel— white robe-like garment worn on Yom Kippur

kiyum— commitment to marry

Klal Yisrael— the Jewish Nation

kneidelach— matzoh balls *(Yiddish)*

kodesh— holy

Kollelim— paid Torah study programs for married men

Koheles— Book of Ecclesiastes written by King Solomon

Korach— Biblical personality, known for his rebellion against Moses

laitzonus— scoffing, joking

lamdon / lamdonim (pl)— accomplished learner

le'fee darko— according to his level (of learning)

lebidicka— lively

levayah— funeral

Limudei Kodesh— religious studies

loshon hara— tale bearing

m'challel Shabbos— profaning the holiness of the Sabbath day

m'chazek— give spiritual and moral strength

m'chutz lamachena— outside of the camp (town)

m'farnes zeh mizeh— to engage in commerce with one another to earn a living

m'kabol panim— to greet someone

Ma'ariv— the evening prayer service

maggid / maggidim (pl)— preacher, lecturer

makom— place

malach hamaves— angel of death

masechta— tractate of Talmud

marktug— market day *(Yiddish)*

mashgiach / mashgichim(pl)—
1. spiritual advisor and mentor of a yeshiva
2. supervisor of kosher food production

maskil / maskilim (pl)— follower of the Enlightenment

mazaldik— lucky or with good fortune

meforshim— Talmudic commentators

melamed / melamdim (pl)— Torah teacher (male)

menachem avel— comfort a mourner

menahel— principal

mentschen— men *(Yiddish)*

mesader kiddushin— person officiating at a marriage

mesiras nefesh— self-sacrifice on behalf of the Torah

mezumin— recited before *bentching* by three or more men who eat together

mezuzah / mezuzos (pl)— small parchments with passages from the Torah, affixed to most doorposts of Jewish houses

midah / midos (pl)— character traits

midbar— desert

mikveh / mikvaos (pl)— ritual bath

min Hashomayim— from heaven

Minchah— Afternoon Prayer Service

mishagas— nonsense *(Yiddish)*

Mishkon— the Tabernacle in the desert

mishloach manos— sending of food portions on Purim

Mishnah Brurah— important books on Jewish law written by the Chofetz Chaim

Mishnayos— books of the Oral Law

Misnagdim— opponents of the Chassidic movement

mistapake b'muat— to be satisfied with little

mitzayer— to pain oneself or grieve

morah / moros (pl)— Torah teacher (female)

Moreinu Rabbeinu— our teacher, our rabbi

Moshiach— the Redeemer, the Messiah

mussar— study of ethical behavior

mussarnicks— adherents to mussar

mye— garden

nedovah— donation

neged hazerem— against the flow

negel vasser— ritual washing of the hands after sleep

Neilah prayer— the last prayer on Yom Kippur

nes— miracle

neshamah / neshamos (pl)— soul

neshamah yeseirah— extra soul acquired by each Jew on the Sabbath

niftar— the deceased

nifter— die

niggun— tune, melody

Ofos— birds; chickens

Olam Haba— the World to Come

Olam Hazeh— This World

Oy Vey— exclamation of concern or distress *(Yiddish)*

parnasah— income, livelihood

pasuk— verse

poritz— gentile landowner

poser chalom— to interpret a dream

potch— slap *(Yiddish)*

prust— crude *(Yiddish)*

Rabos machshavos b'lev ish— "Many thoughts (plans) are in the heart of a man," a Torah quote

rebbe— religious leader or teacher,

rebbetzin— wife of a religious leader or teacher

Rosh Chodesh— beginning of the Jewish month

Rosh Hashanah— the Jewish New Year

Rosh HaYeshiva / Roshei Yeshiva (pl)— dean of the yeshiva

Rov / rabbonim (pl)— Rabbi of a congregation

Ruach Hakodesh— Divine Inspiration

ruchnius— spirituality

schmaltz— fat for cooking

seder / sedorim (pl)— learning session

sefer / seforim (pl)— religious book

seichel— intellect, understanding

seudah— festive meal

shalosh seudos— the third Shabbos meal

Shacharis— Morning Prayer Service

shaluchei mitzvah ainon nizokin— "one who goes to perform a mitzvah is protected from misfortune," a Talmudic teaching

shamosh— synagogue attendant

shecht— to slaughter an animal according to Jewish law

shechitah— ritual slaughter

shem— name (reputation)

Shevat— the eleventh Hebrew month

shidduch— match (for marriage)

shlep— carry *(Yiddish)*

shliach tzibur— person leading the prayer service

shiseleh— pot *(Yiddish)*

shiur / shiurim (pl)—
    1. class   2. lesson

shmues / shmussen (pl)— lecture on ethics and proper conduct

shochet / shochtim (pl)— ritual slaughterer

Shomer Shabbos— Sabbath observer

shtender— lectern *(Yiddish)*

shtetle / shtetlach (pl)— village(s) *(Yid.)*

shtut— place, town *(Yiddish)*

shul— synagogue

Shulchan Aruch— compendium of Jewish law compiled by Rabbi Yosef Caro

Sifrei Torah— Torah scrolls

simchah— joy, joyous occasion

sochrim— businessmen, store owners

sofer / sofrim (pl)— scribe

Succos— the holiday of Tabernacles

taanis dibur— refraining from speaking

tallis— prayer shawl

talmidei chachomim— Torah scholars

talmid / talmidim (pl)— yeshiva student

Talmud— explanation of the Oral Law (Mishnah)

talmud Torah— study of Torah

Tammuz— the fourth Hebrew month

Tanach— books of the Torah, Prophets and Writings

tefillin— phylacteries

Tehillim— the book of Psalms written by King David

tevuah— grain

tog (tug)— day *(Yiddish)*

treif— non-kosher

tzaddik— righteous person

tzedakah— charity and kindness

Tzelem Elokim— image of G-d

tzimmes— a carrot and fruit dish mixed with honey *(Yiddish)*

tzoros— troubles

unterfherers— person(s) accompanying the bride or groom

"v'hu yimshal bah"— "And he will rule over her," a Torah quote

yahrtzeit shiur— a Torah lecture given on the anniversary of one's death

yemach sh'mo— may his name be blotted out

yeshiva/yeshivos— schools where Torah is taught

yeshiva gedolah— religious high school

yeshiva k'tanah— religious elementary school

Yid / Yidden (pl)— Yiddish word for a Jew

yirah— fear, usually associated with fear of Heaven

yiras hakovod— respectful of a parent's honor

Yomim Noraim— Days of Awe

Yom Kippur— Day of Atonement

yom tov— religious holiday

zaidy— grandfather *(Yiddish)*

z'man— A specific amount of time; a school session

zoche b'din— meritorious in judgment

∽ BIBLIOGRAPHY

Encyclopedia Judaica, Jerusalem, Israel, 1978 Edition

Finkelman, Shimon, *Reb Chaim Ozer: The Life and Ideal of Rabbi Chaim Ozer Grodzenski of Vilna*, Mesorah Pub., Brooklyn, NY, 1987

Gilbert, Martin, *The Atlas Of The Holocaust*, William Morrow, New York, NY, 1988

Hertzman, Rabbi Elchonon, *The Mashgiach*, Jerusalem, Israel, 1981

Surasky, Aharon, *Giants of Jewry*, Chinuch Pub., Lakewood, NJ, 1982

Zaitchik, Rabbi Chaim Ephraim, *Sparks Of Mussar*, Feldheim Pub., Spring Valley, New York, 1985

Note: For a comprehensive listing of additional books and related materials, please see page 140

The Student Guide to
THE WORLD THAT WAS: LITHUANIA

Questions, Topics for Research and Discussion,
Activities and Map Exercises

by Rabbi Yitzchak Kasnett, M.S.

QUESTIONS FOR MIR

1. In which country was Mir located before WWII?
2. Under whose jurisdiction was Mir for almost three centuries?
3. What was traded at the Mir Fair?
4. Why was Mir considered an autonomous community?
5. In what year did the Jewish community leaders meet in Mir?
6. What is a poll tax?
7. In what year was the Mir Yeshiva founded and by whom?
8. How many tailors were there in Mir in 1806? Why do you think there were so many more tailors than people involved in other professions?
9. In which years were the Jews the majority in Mir?
10. Who was the last Rov of Mir?
11. When did the Germans capture Mir?
12. Where did they hold the Jews of Mir captive?
13. When did the final destruction of Mir take place?
14. Fill in a blank chart of THE MIRRER YESHIVA from memory.

QUESTIONS FOR TELZ

1. Where is Telz located?
2. What does the term "fascist" mean?
3. What does it mean that Telz was "politically conservative and very attached to Jewish tradition"?
4. When was the yeshiva founded by Rabbi Gordon?
5. What was unique about the Telz community? Explain how this affected the town. How would such a situation affect your city or town?
6. What innovations did Rabbi Gordon introduce into the yeshiva system?
7. Who were the first *Rebbeim* in the yeshiva?
8. What method of teaching did Rabbi Gordon use to deliver his *shiur?* Why would this be an effective way to teach?
9. From the material supplied in this chapter, write a character analysis of Rabbi Gordon, describing his personality and world outlook. Use material from this selection to support your view. Other reference material should be used as well.
10. What was *Knesses Yisrael*? Why was it started and what was its function?
11. List Rabbi Yosef Lieb Bloch's accomplishments, and his reason(s) for taking the actions he did.
12. Who led the remaining Jews of Telz to their deaths at the hands of the Nazis? Describe his behavior at that time.
13. Fill in a blank chart of THE TELZ DYNASTY from memory.
14. Fill in a blank chart of the POPULATION OF TELZ from memory.

Fill in the chart of The Mirrer Yeshiva as presented in your lesson.

Student: _____   Date: _____

Class: _____   Instructor: _____

THE MIRRER YESHIVA

Founded by: _____ : year-
- Rosh HaYeshiva *(son)*
- Rosh HaYeshiva: year-
- Rosh HaYeshiva: year-
- Rosh HaYeshiva: year-
- Rosh HaYeshiva: 19____(son-in-law of _____)

ROSHEI HAYESHIVA OF MIR IN ERETZ YISRAEL:

_____ —

(Evacuated from Lithuania to Eretz Yisrael in 1940, reestablishing the Mirrer Yeshiva in Jerusalem.)

_____ —

(Son-in-law of Rabbi Finkel. Led the Mir to Japan and Shanghai with Rabbi Yechezkel Levenstein ZT"L.)

- Rosh HaYeshiva: 1965

- Rosh HaYeshiva: 1967

Roshei HaYeshiva in 5757/1996:
1. _____
2. _____

ROSHEI HAYESHIVA OF MIR IN AMERICA:

- Rosh HaYeshiva: 1947

- Rosh HaYeshiva: 1947

Roshei HaYeshiva in 5757/1996:
1. _____
2. _____

Student Exercises

Fill in the chart of The Telz Dynasty as presented in your lesson.

Student: _____   Date: _____

Class: _____   Instructor: _____

THE TELZ DYNASTY		
Founded in _____ *by* _____		
Rabbi Eliezer Gordon		
Rabbi Yosef Leib Bloch ( )		
Rabbi Avrohom Yitzchok Bloch ( )		
Rabbi Zalman Bloch ( )		
Rabbi Eliyohu Meir Bloch ( )		
Rabbi Chaim Mordechai Katz ( )		
Rabbi Boruch Sorotzkin ( ) ( )		
Rabbi Mordecai Gifter ( )		
Rabbi Chaim Stein **Rabbi Aizik Ausband** ( ) **Rabbi Pesach Stein** ( )		

Fill in the chart of Population of Telz as presented in your lesson.

Student: _____ Date: _____

Class: _____ Instructor: _____

JEWISH POPULATION OF TELZ
1847-
1864-
1897-   (% of population)
Jewish Population destroyed by the Germans and Lithuanians:
—
1970-

QUESTIONS FOR VILNA

1. Why was 1633 a year of significance for the Jews of Vilna?

2. What is a guild?

3. Why was it important to record "only 12 Jewish shops could be opened to the street"?

4. What investigation did Ladislaus IV commission?

5. In the first half of the 17th century what percentage of the population of Vilna was Jewish?

6. What was the economic situation of the Jews of Vilna in the first half of the 17th century?

7. When did the leadership of Lithuanian Jewry pass to Vilna?

8. Why did the gentiles riot in 1687, and how did the king respond? How much damage was done? Research what that amount would equal in American dollars today.

9. When did the Jewish Quarter in Vilna burn? Who came to their aid?

10. Describe the life of a Vilna Jew throughout most of the 18th Century.

11. Why was Vilna called the Jerusalem of Lithuania?

12. When did the Russians restore autonomy to the Jews of Vilna?

13. How many Jews lived in Vilna and its environs in 1795?

14. When was the existence of Vilna's first Talmud Torah recorded?

15. How many Jews lived in Vilna in 1800?

16. To whom did the Jews give their support in the War of 1812? Write a brief historical report on the background and events of this war, and its effects on the Jews.

17. Write a brief biographical sketch of Czar Nicholas I, and his attitude toward the Jews.

18. In what year was there a large emigration from Vilna, and to which countries did the Jews go?

19. Who led Vilna's Orthodox community in the 20th century?

20. Prepare a chart listing the year and the number of Jews living in Vilna from the information supplied in this chapter.

21. Record your response to the Yom Kippur incident related by Rabbi Graubart.

22. How did Reb Chaim Ozer respond to the needs of his Jewish brethren during the years of WWI?

23. What did Reb Chaim Ozer find upon his return to Vilna after WWI? Explain.

EXTENSION EXERCISES FOR HISTORY SECTION

1. Present the plan of action you would take if you had to negotiate relief aid for the Jews of a foreign and hostile country. The following are some of the things you will need to consider:
    A. Whose aid would you enlist?
    B. How would you approach the various officials?
    C. What arguments would you present?
    D. How would you organize support for this relief effort?
    E. How would you get supplies to those who need it?

    ❑   Write a detailed plan including the names of current government officials, leaders of the Jewish world and any international political/social organizations relevant to your cause. Produce lists of materials, funds, etc., including maps showing the rescue routes (if needed) to be employed. Alternative plans of rescue should be discussed and delineated in case of emergency. It would be best to prepare this plan in groups of 3 to 5 students.

2. Research the life of Czar Nicholas II and his attitude and behavior towards the Jews of Russia.

3. Prepare a book report on any of the following historical biographies:
    (See page 140 for additional titles)

    ❑   **Operation: Torah Rescue** *(Feldheim)*

    ❑   **The Story of Reb Chaim Ozer** *(ArtScroll)*

    ❑   **A Fire in His Soul** *(Feldheim Pub)*

    ❑   **Reb Elchonon** *(ArtScroll)*

    ❑   **The Rosh Yeshiva** *(Targum-Feldheim)*

    ❑   **Holocaust Diaries Collection** *(CIS)*

4. Research the founding and history of two of the following yeshivas:

Baranovich	Mir
Bialistock	Novardok
Brisk	Pinsk
Grodno	Ponovezh
Kaminetz	Radin
Kelm	Slabodka
Kletzk	Slonim
Kobrin	Telz
Lomza	Volozhin
Lublin	

5. Write a historical review of the effects of World War I on the Jews of Eastern Europe. This is a very broad topic, therefore, you may speak with your instructor to decide on a more specific aspect of this question to research.

6. Draw comparative maps of Europe over the last 150 years showing how the boundaries of the countries on the European continent changed (time and again) during that period. What do you think it would be like to have lived in Europe during any of the periods of turmoil and change, when territories from the various countries were lost or gained by armed conflict or otherwise? Explain how you think this would affect your life as an individual, the lives of your family members (infants to the elderly), and, finally, the life of your community.

7. After World War II, Rabbi Eliezer Silver went to Eastern Europe as the head of the *Vaad Hatzala*, to see what he could do to relieve the suffering of the Jews who had survived the war. Assume that you are the representative of a similar organization who is arriving in Vilna with the return of Reb Chaim Ozer at the end of WWI. Try to imagine what the refugees would have felt and thought upon hearing that an American, the head of a large relief agency, is present to listen and give assistance? Write a page in your diary recounting the events of that day. Before beginning this exercise make a list of the services you would like to render, and the supplies you would bring.

8. Conduct your own interview of a relative or neighbor who lived in Europe before World War II. Prepare questions for them to answer in a live interview in front of the class. Alternatively, prepare a report of the interview for presentation to the class.

QUESTIONS FOR THE INTERVIEW WITH RABBI GIFTER, SHLITA

1. What could you do to "de-fragment" your life so that Torah became the consciousness that directed all areas of your activities.

2. What main teaching did Reb Yosef Leib impart to his *talmidim* and to *Klal Yisrael*?

3. What thoughts lie behind Reb Meisel's business outlook?

4. What does the statement, "This was the feeling one had in Telz—you belonged, it was home" mean to you? Explain.

QUESTIONS FOR THE INTERVIEW WITH RABBI MILLER, SHLITA

1. Rabbi Miller mentions that some of the older *bochurim* never married because of World War I and the social/political upheaval that followed. Describe the situation that existed at the time and why it made the lives of so many Jews extremely difficult.

2. What does it mean to behave in a "frivolous manner"?

3. How does Rabbi Miller explain the concept of *Tzelem Elokim?*

4. What did the Alter mean when he said, "We want to make them great, but they won't let us make them great"?

5. Why is it important to control your tongue?

6. Explain why it is easy to destroy one's spiritual accomplishments.

7. Describe who the Bolsheviks were, their origin and what they represented.

8. How did Reb Isaac Sher explain the passage mentioned in the *Mesillas Yeshorim?* First try to review this passage from the *sefer* itself.

9. Why did Reb Isaac not speak about *Gehinnom* to the boys in Slabodka?

10. Explain the principle or awareness stated by Rabbi Miller as one important to the Jewish youth of today, and why it is of such importance.

11. Explain what you perceive to be the main attitude expressed by Rabbi Miller throughout his interview.

12. Which incident most affected Rabbi Miller's growth and development as a young man? Explain.

13. Describe an incident that changed you as a person.

14. Rabbi Miller is a very well-known Torah personality living in Brooklyn, New York. Write a brief description of his accomplishments.

15. What part of this interview interested you the most?

Fill in the chart of The Slabodka Yeshiva as presented in your lesson.

Student: _____   Date: _____

Class: _____   Instructor: _____

THE SLABODKA YESHIVA AND ITS INFLUENCE

Founded in _____ *by* _____ *, a.k.a.* "_____"

Rabbi Nosson Tzvi Finkel ( )	
Reb Yitzchok Yaakov Rabinowitz a.k.a." "	
Rabbi Isser Zalman Meltzer	
Rabbi Moshe Mordechai Epstein	
Rabbi Yitzchok Isaac Sher ( )	

Influence of "_____" and the Slabodka Derech on European Yeshivos

Telz Yeshiva	
Slutsk Yeshiva	
Mirrer Yeshiva	
Stuchin/Anaf Knesses Yisrael	
Kobrin Yeshiva	
Kletzk Yeshiva	

Influence of "_____" and the Slabodka Derech on American Yeshivos

Beis Medrash Gevoah/Lakewood	
Yeshiva Rabbi Chaim Berlin	
Yeshiva Torah Vodaath	
Yeshiva Ner Yisrael/Baltimore	
Yeshiva Chofetz Chaim	
Beis Yisroel Torah Center	

QUESTIONS FOR THE INTERVIEW WITH RABBI DESSLER, SHLITA

1. What lesson did Rabbi Dessler's grandfather teach him about people?

2. What experience did the Lomza *Mashgiach* have in Kelm? How did this incident symbolize life in Kelm?

3. What was the main preoccupation of the students in the Kelm Talmud Torah? What examples of this are provided by Rabbi Dessler?

4. *Chazal* say that a person needs *daled amos* (4 *amos* by 4 *amos*) of personal space. Let's use the measure of 2 feet to an *amah*. How many square feet does *daled amos* equal? If there were 25 men learning in the Talmud Torah, and the building was 45' by 60', how much space was there for each of the students? What conclusions can you make from the amount of space each man occupied?

5. List the four Torah giants mentioned in the interview who learned in Kelm.

6. What lesson do we learn from the story about how Reb Nochum Zev ate?

7. What is important about the fact that Reb Simcha Zissel's family had lived in Kelm for 12 or 13 generations?

8. Who was Rabbi Dessler's father? Grandfather, Great-grandfather? Great-great-grandfather?

9. How did Rabbi Dessler's childhood differ from your own?

10. Did you ever hear anything like the story Rabbi Dessler related about his walk with his grandmother? Why is it necessary for an American Jew to hear such a story? What personal lessons did you derive from it?

11. In your own words, describe the spiritual and material life that the Jews of Kelm lived. Include examples from the interview.

12. Why was Reb Simcha Zissel's book bindery left untouched?

13. Write a newspaper article for your local newspaper explaining the court case in Kelm, where one tries to sell for less and the other tries to buy for more. How do you think the average American reader would respond to such an article? Would he think it was a joke?

14. Today people keep their stores open for set hours. What considerations did Nechama Leiba have that caused her to run her store as she did?

15. Could the incident with the cane take place today? Why or why not.

16. What influences, positive and/or negative, most affect our attitudes and commitment to religion today in America?

17. What is so frustrating about the incident with the American Consulate?

18. Explain why the lesson of the rubles is so important for life in America?

19. How can you apply the lesson of the "bus stop" in your own life. List examples.

20. Write a detailed plan how you would train yourself, or someone else, to live by the dictates of the mind and common sense, and not one's desires.

21. What sustained Rabbi Dessler's spiritual life in Kelm, and what limits it here?

22. How do you relate to the sleeping conditions in Telz?

STUDENT WORKSHEET FOR THE INTERVIEW WITH REBBETZIN GINSBURG

Student: _____ **Date**: _____

Before reading the interview with Rebbetzin Ginsburg, you are to write the ideas, concepts, main points or other important information that represents your thoughts, feelings and how meaningful each of the following issues is to you.

This Worksheet is being completed from the perspective of the:

❏ **Student**   ❏ **Rebbetzin**

1. What principles do you live for?

2. List the ten most important things in your life.

3. What concerns come to mind when you consider the meaning of marriage?

4. When you think about planning a wedding, what issues and concerns come to mind?

5. What is true wealth to you?

6. Are you rich or poor? What do these terms mean to you?

7. List ten things for which you are grateful to Hashem.

8. Luxuries: what can you just not live without?

9. List five things that you feel are missing from your life.

10. What are your three biggest praises about life?

11. What are your three biggest complaints about life?

12. What does it mean for you to be well-mannered and well-behaved?

After you finish reading the Interview with Rebbetzin Ginsburg, fill out this work sheet again, only this time from her perspective of the issues. Where there is no direct comment by the Rebbetzin concerning her feelings and thoughts on these issues, project what you think she might say based on her thoughts overall. When you finish, compare your answers.

Student Exercises

QUESTIONS FOR THE INTERVIEW WITH REBBETZIN GINSBURG

(The instructor is encouraged to prepare additional questions and exercises from the interview)

1. Write a brief biography of Rabbi Yisroel Salanter, including a listing of his chief disciples.

2. Explain what is meant by the phrase that one's faith is "ingrained like the reflex of removing one's hand from a flame?"

3. Familiarize yourself with the location of the major yeshivas and Jewish towns in Lithuania as indicated by your teacher. Be prepared to fill in a blank map with the location of each yeshiva.

4. Speak with someone who is familiar with the steps involved in properly koshering a chicken. Write directions for the preparation of a chicken (according to Jewish Law), from purchase to table, as Jews did in Europe when the Rebbetzin was a child. How long did it take to prepare one chicken then?

5. How deep underground is the water table in your area? How many feet would you have to drill to install a pump next to your house? Most cities have companies that drill wells. Call one and see if you can get the answer to this question. Also, what is the cost?

6. Take a large pail of water and carry it back and forth across the street in front of your house several times. When you have finished doing this, write a paragraph describing your appreciation for having running water in the house.

7. Map out the amount of living space the Rebbetzin had in an area of your own house and describe what it would be like for you and your family to use only that much living space for one week. How many square feet is your house or apartment? Measure all of the rooms and find out. How much greater is the square footage of your home than that of the Rebbetzin?

8. Turn off the heat in your room on a cold winter's night and sit and try to read or study as the temperature drops. How does such a situation affect your ability to concentrate and study? Describe what it is like to walk out of your room into the one right next door that has heat. Try this for as long a period of time as you can without threatening your health. It is particularly effective to try this exercise on very cold mornings.

9. Take a bucket of water and leave it outside on a very cold winter's night when the temperature is well below freezing. In the morning retrieve the bucket and use its contents for all of your washing and cooking needs. After you have finished, write down a step-by-step description of how you managed the situation and what you did. Finally, compare this condition with that of having hot and cold running water in your house.

10. How long does it take you to fill your tub with hot water for a bath? Next, take a large pot and estimate (or actually measure) how many such potfulls of water you would need to fill your tub. Then estimate how long it would take to heat-up that amount of water on the oven. Once you have completed all of this, estimate how long it would take you to prepare a bath from the drawing of the water at the well until it is finally heated and ready for use. If you had to prepare a bath in this manner every time you bathed, how often do you think you would bathe each week?

11. Sit down with your father and/or mother and discuss how to arrange the family affairs so that he or she could take off work for about six weeks (from *Rosh Chodesh Elul* until after Yom Kippur) and go to a yeshiva or seminary to learn. Discuss how the family would manage its affairs, to whom each responsibility would be delegated, and how you think such a situation would affect the family members. When you finish your discussion, commit it to paper so that you can compare and share the plans, outlook and responses of your family with that of other families in the class.

12. List at least three situations where you could apply the teaching of Rabbi Levenstein, that it is necessary to go against the flow, *neged hazerem,* to your own life. For each case, explain how responding in such a manner would benefit you now and in the future.

13. Consider how you spend the month of *Elul* preparing for Rosh Hashanah. How does the Rebbetzin describe her father's preparations? Make a list of 5 to 10 things you could do to improve your preparations during this month. This may be something you would want to discuss with your Rebbe or Morah.

14. What are your feelings regarding Rebbetzin Ginsburg's reflections on the differences in *chasunahs* in Eastern Europe before the war and in America now? On which points do you agree with her, and on which points do you disagree? Compose your thoughts in an essay that helps you examine and clarify your thoughts on this issue.

15. The Rebbetzin comments that life in Eastern Europe was more *kodesh*, more holy. In what ways can you make your life one that is more *kodesh*?

16. For the boys—how many of these items do you own:
    pairs of pants, shirts, suits, coats and pairs of shoes?

    For the girls--how many of these items do you own:
    dresses, skirts, blouses, coats and pairs of shoes?

    Did you know you had this many of each article?
    How would someone from Kelm, in 1920, feel about owning such a wardrobe? How would you feel owning the amount of clothes the Rebbetzin did? How would this change your life? Explain.

17. Write a short biography of Sara Schenirer and present it to the class.

18. What is *derech eretz,* and do you consider yourself to be a *ba'al derech eretz*? Do you agree with the Rebbetzin's observations regarding *derech eretz*? In what ways do you think you could improve your *derech eretz* towards your parents, friends and strangers?

19. Research the *Roshei Yeshiva*, *Mashgiach* and *Rebbaim* of the yeshivas of Kletzk and Radin. Describe their styles of learning, and what they were like in general.

20. Who was the *Rosh Yeshiva* of the Lomza Yeshiva and when was it founded?

21. Write a brief historical summary of the political changes in Eastern and Western Europe, and Russia, from 1989 until 1993.

22. Write a brief biography of the famous Mirrer *Mashgiach,* Rabbi Yeruchem Levovitz, *zt"l.* Be sure to include a list of his writings.

23. Record your impression of Rabbi Levenstein in light of his decision to remain in Kelm and take care of his mother-in-law, rather than join Rabbi Aharon Kotler, *zt"l,* at his yeshiva in Kletzk. Do you think you would act similarly should an important position be offered to you?

24. Regarding her flight from Danzig into Poland, the Rebbetzin questions the reader and asks, "Can you imagine doing that?" Can you? Explain your thoughts and emotions concerning the possibility of being subjected to such a trying experience.

25. The Rebbetzin relates that her house in Kelm sold for $1,200. How much would that amount be worth now given the current value of the dollar?

26. If you used only the products that the Rebbetzin used for *Pesach*, how much would you need to spend to make *Pesach*? How great a savings would that be over what you spend now? Would you enjoy *Pesach* as much? Explain.

27. Explain the three different levels in the yeshiva system in Eastern Europe.

EXTENSION EXERCISES:
INTERVIEW WITH REBBETZIN GINSBURG

1. Interview one of your older relatives about their childhood and youth. First write at least 15 to 20 "starter" questions to get the interview going and the interviewee talking and comfortable.

2. Write a character sketch of Rebbetzin Ginsburg. Include your overall impression of the Rebbetzin, her nature and personality, and what most impresses you about her. Cite material presented in the interview to substantiate your point of view.

3. What part of the interview interested you the most? Explain why.

4. You have read how the Mirrer Yeshiva was plucked from the flames of destruction. If you were among that group, how would the events you went through influence the rest of your life? What do you think you would do with yourself after reaching the United States? Commit your thoughts to an essay examining the issues involved in this question. It might be helpful for your instructor to discuss this question with the class to assist you to identify the relevant issues you need to include.

MAP SKILLS: EUROPE BEFORE WORLD WAR II

Student: _____   Date: _____

Class: _____   Instructor: _____

Fill in the names of the countries indicated on this map.

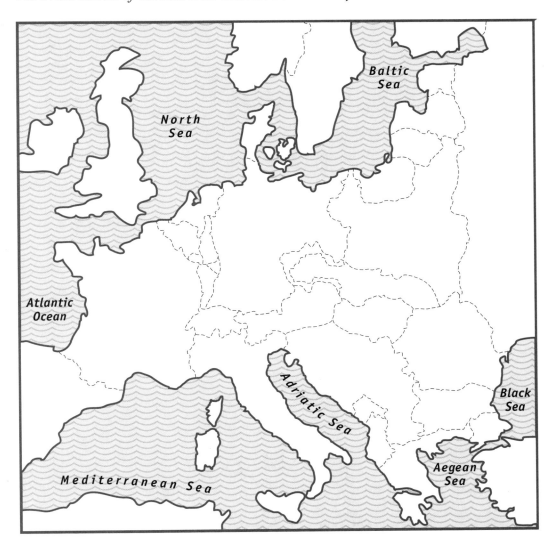

MAP SKILLS

Student: _____   **Date:** _____

Class: _____   **Instructor:** _____

Fill in the locations of the yeshivos.

MAP SKILLS

Student: _____   Date: _____

Class: _____   Instructor: _____

Fill in the locations of the cities and countries where Reb Chatzkel and his family journeyed. Also fill in the legend box.

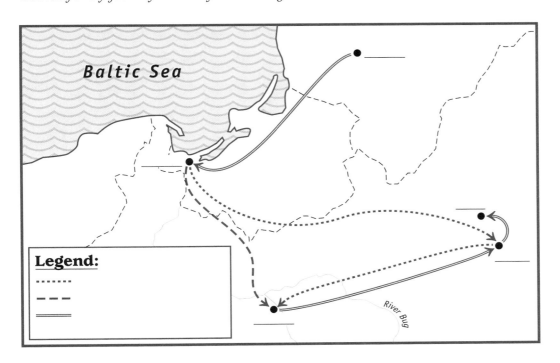

Baltic Sea

Legend:

· · · · · · ·

— — —

══════

River Bug

MAP SKILLS *(page 1 of spread)*

Student: _____ Date: _____

Class: _____ Instructor: _____

Fill in the location of the cities along the escape route of the Mirrer Yeshiva. Also fill in the legend box.

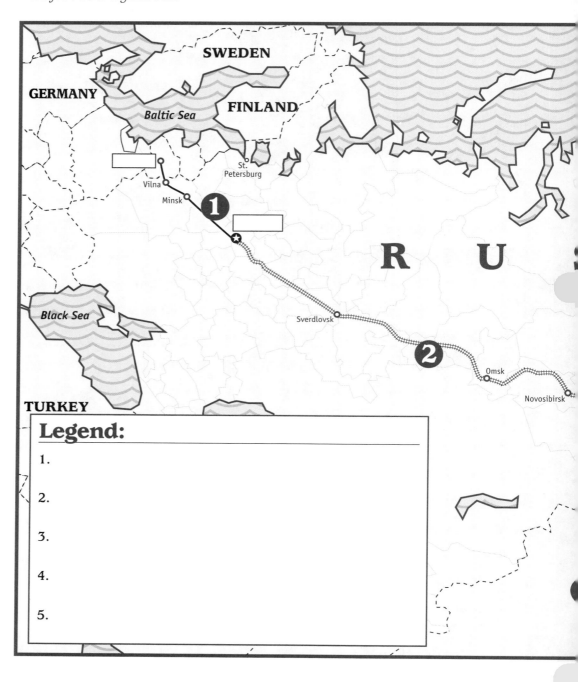

MAP SKILLS *(page 2 of spread)*

Student: _____ Date: _____

Class: _____ Instructor: _____

Fill in the location of the cities along the escape route of the Mirrer Yeshiva.

RECOMMENDED READING AND SOURCE MATERIAL

here are many resources not listed here that are available on various aspects of the Holocaust (children, concentration and labor camps, diaries, biographies, historical essays, politics, etc.), including audio-video and interactive classroom materials. **It is strongly recommended that these materials be reviewed by an appropriate school official before being introduced within the classroom.** Many of these resources contain shocking and frightening contents, including pictures of naked and mutilated bodies, that should not be viewed by children. Additionally, many are published by various groups bearing their own perspective of the Holocaust, often in contradiction with a Torah point of view. It is strongly suggested that even the material listed in this bibliography be reviewed for specific age appropriateness before being introduced in the classroom.

CIS PUBLICATIONS

180 Park Ave., Lakewood, New Jersey 08702 — 908-905-3000

Holocaust Diaries Collection

Banet, Chana Marcus, *They Called Me Frau Anna*, 1990

Eilenberg, Anna, *Sisters In The Storm*, 1992

Friedman, Chaim Shlomo, *Dare To Survive*, 1992

Gabel, Dina, *Behind The Ice Curtain*, 1992

Holczler, Moshe, *Late Shadows*, 1989

Kacenberg, Mala, *Alone in the Forest*, 1995

Krakowski, Avraham, *Counterfeit Lives*, 1994

Pomerantz, Yitzchak, *Itzik, Be Strong!*, 1993

Sanik, Leibel, *Someday We'll Be Free*, 1994

Werdyger, Duvid, *Songs of Hope*, 1993

Other Related Publications from CIS

Alfasi, Yitzchak, *Glimpses Of Jewish Warsaw*, 1992

Alfasi, Yitzchak, *Glimpses Of Jewish Frankfurt*, 1993

Beilis, Mendel, *Scapegoat On Trial*, 1992

Chazan, Aaron, *Deep In The Russian Night*, 1990

Eibeshitz, Y. and A., *Women In The Holocaust*, Volumes 1 & 2, 1994

Gevirtz, E. and Kranzler, D., *To Save A World*, Volumes 1 & 2, 1991

Pomerantz, Rachel, *Wings Above The Flames*, 1992

Pomerantz, Rachel, *The World In Flames*, 1993

Winston, Rabbi Pinchas, *The Eternal Link*, 1990

Winston, Rabbi Pinchas, *The Unbroken Chain of Jewish Tradition*, 1986

FELDHEIM PUBLISHERS

200 Airport Executive Park, Suite 202, Spring Valley, New York 10954 — 914-356-2282

Allswang, Dr. Benzion, *The Final Resolution*, 1989

Araten, Rochel Sarna, *Michalina: Daughter Of Israel*, 1986

Baumol, Rav Yehoshua, *A Blaze in the Darkening Gloom*, 1994

Benisch, Pearl, *To Vanquish The Dragon*, 1991

Bunim, Amos, *A Fire In His Soul*, 1989

Firer, Benzion, *The Twins*, 1981

Fox, David, *Greatness In Our Midst*, 1955

Glicksman, Devorah, *A Sun And A Shield*, 1996

Granatstein, Yechiel, *One Jew's Power-One Jew's Glory*, 1991

Grossman, Rav Reuven, *The Legacy Of Slabodka*, 1989

Grossman, Rav Reuven, *The Rosh Yeshiva*, 1988

Kahn, Betzalel, *Citadel Of Splendor*, 1995

Klein, R.L., *The Scent Of Snowflowers*, 1989

Lamet, Rosalie, *City Of Diamonds*, 1996

Leitner, Yecheskel, *Operation: Torah Rescue*, 1987

Rakeffet-Rothkoff, Aaron, *The Silver Era*, 1988

Schleimer, Sarah M., *Far From The Place We Called Home*, 1994

Schiff, Rabbi Elyakim and G., *The Five Gates*, 1994

Shain, Ruchoma, *All For The Boss*, 1984

Shapiro, Chaim, *Go, My Son*, 1989

Sinason, Jacob H., *Saba Marches On*, 1993

Sonnenfeld, S. Z., *Voices In The Silence*, 1992

Unsdorfer, Simcha Bunim, *The Yellow Star*, 1983

Zaitchik, Rabbi Chaim Ephraim, *Sparks Of Mussar*, 1985

Student Exercises

JUDAICA PRESS
123 Ditmas Ave, Brooklyn, New York 11218 — 718-972-6200

Oshry, Rabbi Ephraim, *Responsa From The Holocaust*, 1983

Oshry, Rabbi Ephraim, *The Annihilation Of Lithuanian Jewry*, 1996

MESORAH PUBLICATIONS, LTD.
4401 Second Ave, Brooklyn, New York 11232 — 718-921-9000

Birnbaum, Meyer, *Lieutenant Birnbaum*, 1993

Bromberg, Rabbi Y.A., *The Sanzer Rav And His Dynasty*, 1986

Dansky, Miriam, *Rebbetzin Grunfeld*, 1994

Finkelman, Shimon, *Reb Chaim Ozer-The Life and Ideal of Rabbi Chaim Ozer Grodzenski of Vilna*, 1987

Finkelman, Shimon, *The Chazon Ish*, 1989

Finkelman, Shimon, *Reb Moshe*, 1986

Friedenson, Joseph, *Dateline: Istanbul*, 1993

Friedenson, J. and Kranzler, D., *Heroine Of Rescue*, 1984

Friedman, Peska, *Going Forward*, 1994

Fuchs, Abraham, *The Unheeded Cry*, 1984

Gottlieb, N.Z., *In The Shadow Of The Kremlin*, 1985

Granatstein, Yechiel, *The War Of A Jewish Partisan*, 1986

Kranzler, David, *Thy Brother's Blood*, 1987

Pekier, Alter, *From Kletzk to Siberia*, 1985

Prager, Moshe, *Sparks Of Glory*, 1985

Rosenblum, Yonason, *The Vilna Gaon*, 1994

Rosenblum, Yonasan, *They Called Him Mike*, 1995

Rosenblum, Yonason, *Reb Yaakov*, 1993

Rubin, Chana Stavsky, *Tomorrow May Be Too Late*, 1995

Schwartz, Rabbi Y. and Goldstein, Y., *Shoah*, 1990

Sorasky, Aaron, *Reb Elchonon*, 1982

Wahrman, Rabbi Shlomo, *Lest We Forget*, 1991

Wein, Rabbi Berel, *Triumph Of Survival*, 1990

Wolpin, Rabbi Nisson, *A Path Through The Ashes*, 1986

Wolpin, Rabbi Nisson, *The Torah Profile*, 1988

Wolpin, Rabbi Nisson, *The Torah Personality*, 1980

Wolpin, Rabbi Nisson, *The Torah World*, Brooklyn, 1982

Wolpin, Rabbi Nisson, *Torah Luminaries*, 1994

Wolpin, Nisson, *Torah Lives,* 1995

Worch, Renee, *Flight*, 1988

Worch, Renee, *Survival*, 1992

Yosher, Rabbi Moses, *The Chafetz Chaim*, 1984

Zakon, Miriam Stark, *Silent Revolution*, 1988

WILLIAM MORROW AND COMPANY, INC.

1350 Avenue of the Americas, New York, New York 10019 — 800-843-9389

Gilbert, Martin, *The Atlas Of The Holocaust*, 1988

Gilbert, Martin, *The Atlas Of Jewish History*, 1969

VINTAGE BOOKS

400 Hahn Road, Westminster, Maryland 21157 — 800-733-3000

Eliach, Yaffa, *Hasidic Tales Of The Holocaust*, 1988

BOOKS FROM OTHER PUBLISHERS

Encyclopedia Judaica, Jerusalem, Israel, 1978 Edition

Ganz, Yaffa, *Sand and Stars (Vol II),* Shaar Press, Monsey, NY, 1995 (distributor Mesorah)

Hertzman, Rabbi Elchonon, *The Mashgiach*, Jerusalem, Israel, 1981

Salamander, Rachel, *The Jewish World of Yesterday*, Rizzoli, NY, 1991 (distributor CIS)

Surasky, Aharon, *Giants of Jewry*, Chinuch Pub., Lakewood, NJ, 1982

Wein, Berel, *Truimph of Survival,* Shaar Press, Monsey, NY, 1990 (distributor Mesorah)

JACKDAW PUBLICATIONS (A Division of Golden Owl Publishing)

P.O. Box 503, Amawalk, New York 10501 — 800-789-0022 or 914-962-6911

The Holocaust **(an interactive classroom materials kit)**